The COSt

*Creation was corrupted by Adam's
Original Sin which Separated
man from God requiring that we be
✝ (the Cross) redeemed with our Creator.*

*Why old earth (death before Adam) beliefs
undermine faith in the Gospel
and the knowledge
needed to defend biblical
faith.*

By Russ Miller

International Standard Book
Number ISBN
9781507531952

Book Cover By Rich Zinzer

Cover Photo: Robert Tewart

Produced in the United States of America Creation,
Evolution & Science Ministries Publications
Gilbert, AZ 85296

Publisher's Note

Have you ever wondered why m a n y Secularists spend so much time attacking Christians and Biblical concepts if they do not believe they are true? Why would they care so passionately? It is because if God's Word is true, especially with regard to the six-day creation and the global Flood, their foundations (*billions of years leading to mankind through a Darwinian-style process*) are destroyed.

Bible-based Christianity stands opposed to the secular worldview. This forces tolerance-proselytizing Secularists to make a huge exception to their paradigm. I refer to this exception as **ABC Tolerance: Anything But Christianity**.

The Secular agenda is simple: Destroy people's faith in biblical Christianity by undermining their faith in the Bible's foundations. They know if they can get a person to believe that Genesis is a myth or allegory, those people will not understand why it matters whether they accept Jesus for the Creator and Judge He claims to be. Then those people might accept non-biblical versions of Jesus or simply reject Him as one of a thousand false deities being worshipped around the world.

I refer to the biblical foundations, which are laid down in Genesis 1 and 3, as the **COSt**. This stands for God's perfect **(C)**reation that was corrupted by Adam's **(O)**riginal Sin which **(S)**eparated mankind from God (while allowing death to enter the world) requiring that we be **†** (the Cross of Christ) redeemed with our loving Creator who is also our redeeming Savior, Lord Jesus the Christ.

The **COSt** is the foundation of the Gospel message. Beliefs that place death prior to the arrival of mankind are in direct conflict with these biblical foundations. Time beyond human comprehension makes the impossible become possible in the minds of those who desire to exchange the truth of God for a lie. *Billions of years* of time is an idea that has provided the foundation for Darwinism, Naturalism and Secular Humanism.

Old-earth tenets are based on the starting presupposition that the earth is *billions of years* old, and that it was *billions of years* of death that brought man into existence. Because most people only hear the secular interpretation of the universe, *billions of years* beliefs have been used to undermine the faith of billions of people in the Gospel message.

Most Christians who have accepted one of the various old-earth philosophies are unaware of the biblical foundations. This book will help them to understand the **COST** so they can perceive how old-earth beliefs, which place death prior to Adam, undermine the **COST**. Only then can a person truly grasp why the *age of the earth* issues matter.

Colossians 2:8 *Beware lest any man spoil you through philosophy and vain deceit, after the tradition of men, after the rudiments of the world, and not after Christ.*

God willing, this book will help those who are seeking the Truth.

About the Author

After building a successful business, Russ Miller gave it away to begin Creation Evolution & Science Ministries. A former Theistic Evolutionist, Russ now ministers to Christians and non-Christians alike, stating, "I'm a General Manager and I make logical decisions based on facts. After I realized that observation-based science does not support Darwinism or old-earth beliefs I decided to do something to help people who have been misled by such false knowledge."

Russ has developed CESM's popular messages, DVD's, Grand Canyon & Grand Staircase tours, radio programs and website. He has also authored five books and two activity books for kids.

Russ has shared in churches across the nation and spoken alongside Ken Ham, Duane Gish, John Morris, Ray Comfort, Eric Hovind, Francis Chan, Josh McDowell, Frank Peretti, Chuck Missler, Carl Baugh, Dave Reagan, Gary Parker and other Godly men. He has also spoken on college campuses and appeared on many Christian television programs.

Russ adds, "Our mission is to confirm biblical Truth and expose misinterpretations of God's Creation in order to exalt Jesus Christ as our Creator, Judge, and redeeming Savior."

The COSt
God Created, Sin Separated,
Christ paid the COSt at
the Cross

Section I:
The Top Ten Old-Earth Beliefs
Compared to Scientific Facts and the
Biblical Worldview

Section II:
The Top Ten Evil Fruits of Old-Earth Beliefs

- ### Including the Top Ten Darwinian Beliefs

Section III:
Ten Reasons To Believe God's Word: Creation Compared to Science and the Secular Worldview

Section IV:
What We Can Do

FORWARD

In the beginning God created the heaven and the earth.
Genesis 1:1

The first sentence of the first verse in the first chapter of the first book of the Bible is plain and simple. God created in the beginning.

And God saw everything that he had made, and, behold, it was very good. And the evening and the morning were the sixth day. Genesis 1:31

According to God, His creation, completed in six days, was *very good* according to His perfect and righteous judgment.

After the creation event, and the seventh day of rest, the Bible reveals what happened to His Creation and why Jesus' death on the cross was made necessary in what I refer to as the **COS†**. The **COS†** represents the foundations of biblical Christianity: God's perfect **(C)**reation was corrupted by Adam's **(O)**riginal Sin which **(S)**eparated mankind from God (while allowing death to enter the world) requiring we be redeemed † (the Cross of Christ) with our loving Creator who is also our redeeming Savior, Lord Jesus the Christ.

The world is collapsing around us, which is what we should expect of a fallen and cursed Creation. We see societies in chaos everywhere we look: moral collapse, economic woes, anti-Christian bias in the media and in America's public schools, eroding freedoms, earthquakes, pestilences, wars and rumors of wars... there seems to be no end to the list.

The problems seem so overwhelming that many Christians throw in the towel. But Believers are told to contend for the faith, not to quit. In order to contend effectively, we must scrutinize the situation, locate the main problem, and identify the key foundational issues involved. This is actually fairly simple to accomplish. In fact, it is so simple that accepting the solution is a challenge to some folks.

We have already scrutinized the situation. Next comes identifying the primary problem and this is not too hard to do. Much of the world's population has lost faith in the authority of God's Word. So, we need to ask ourselves one question: Why?

In case you have not noticed, we are involved in a war between two opposing worldviews. This war began in the Garden of Eden and will end when the Lion of Judah returns to reclaim His Creation. In modern terminology the two views are:

1] **the biblical worldview** based on the **COS†**: that God's perfect **C**reation was corrupted by Adam's **O**riginal sin which **S**eparated us from our loving Creator, requiring our **†** redemption with God through acceptance of our redeeming Savior, Jesus Christ; and

2] **the secular worldview** based on *billions of years leading to Darwinism.*

Old-earth tenets are based on the starting presupposition that the earth, death and suffering existed for *billions of years* **before** man came along.

Well, if *billions of years* of death brought man into existence there would have been no original sin that brought death into the world while separating us from our Creator. In turn, there would be no need for Jesus' redeeming sacrifice on the cross – even if 90% of Christians who compromise God's Word with one of the various old-earth philosophies don't realize it.

Beware lest any man spoil you through philosophy and vain deceit, after the tradition of men, after the rudiments of the world, and not after Christ. Colossians 2:8

The truth is that if *billions of years* leading to mankind is true then God's Word is not true. Thus we need to determine which worldview fits the facts.

Since the secular worldview is taught as if it were science around the globe, I certainly understand why much of the world's population has lost faith in the authority of God's Word. On the other hand, if Scripture is true then *billions of years leading to mankind* is not true and billions of people have been misled. And the war of opposing worldviews rages on.

So how can we believe the Bible and be scientific at the same time? Do old-earth beliefs really compromise God's Word? Are old-earth beliefs a scientific fact? Is there any reliable proof of a worldwide Flood? The following chapters will reveal the answers to these questions and many more.

The primary battle in the war of worldviews is easy to see. We were either created by God or we evolved without any god. This is the reason the secular attack is focused on the very first verse of the very first book of the Bible.

This is where the battle begins and ends. Because of this, if we identify the foundational issues of the *creation versus evolution* battle, we will be able to effectively contend for the faith.

Ask yourself, what is the foundation for Secular Humanism? The answer is Naturalism. So what is the foundation for Naturalism? The answer is Darwinism. And what is the foundation of Darwinism? Its foundation is *billions of years* of time.

I will explain how old-earth beliefs are derived in the following chapters. As you will learn from this book, old-earth beliefs are based on another belief; the earth's crust, the sedimentary layers of rock, formed slowly over vast ages of time rather than quickly during a global flood.

As simple as this sounds, it boils down to whether or not God judged His Creation with a flood of waters that covered all the high hills under heaven. The worldwide deluge is a lynch pin in the war of worldviews.

Okay. We have scrutinized the situation, identified the main problem, and located the key foundational issue involved. Unfortunately, accepting the solution is a challenge to many people because:
a) what seems so overwhelming is really fairly easy to understand, and
b) old-earth beliefs are deeply engrained throughout secular society (it is their foundation) and sadly, within the institutionalized Christian Church.

This should identify *billions of years* beliefs as the key issues that they are. Time is the glue that holds Atheists, Humanists, Theistic Evolutionists, Progressive Creationists, New Agers and Gap Theorists together.

During 1962-1963, secular opportunists succeeded in getting the Supreme Court to replace prayer and biblical Creation in America's public schools with the foundational beliefs of Humanism, *billions of years leading to Darwinism.*

Secular geologists adamantly deny the world endured a global Flood. They have no other choice, as such an event explains how the earth's crust formed quickly, destroying their religious foundation of long ages of time. This in turn undermines Darwinism, which then undermines Humanism. It really is about whether or not there was a global Flood.

The Apostle Paul warned in 1 Timothy 6:20-21,

O Timothy, keep that which is committed to thy trust, avoiding profane and vain babblings, and oppositions of science falsely so called: Which some professing have erred concerning the faith.

Erred concerning the faith?

The word *science*, according to Strong's Lexicon, is a translation of the Greek word *gnosis – knowledge.* Paul wrote this at a time when Gnostics were employing lies, false knowledge, to undermine people's faith in the one true God. Today, Secular Humanists use false knowledge to undermine people's faith in the one true God as they promote their foundational philosophy, *billions of years leading to Darwinism*, as if it were science. This has indeed caused many people to err concerning their faith.

The Bible tells how we came to be, why we are here, and how everything will end. The Bible is the true history book of the universe, and the worldwide Flood during the days of Noah washes away old-earth beliefs. This leaves God's uncompromised Word as the only viable explanation for our existence, and of our future. Only by understanding how *old earth* beliefs place death prior to Adam, undermining the **COST**, can a person truly grasp why the *age of the earth* issues matter.

In the pages that follow, I will explore the world we live in and compare the observable facts to both the secular and the biblical worldviews. I will also suggest some logical courses of action to take. I exhort you to not throw in the towel! The Truth is on the side of the Believer, and as we are told in Romans 8:31,

...If God be for us, who can be against us?

Section I:
The Top Ten Old-Earth Beliefs Compared to Scientific Facts and the Biblical Worldview

Introduction to Chapters 1 -6

Real science, knowledge derived from the study of observable evidence, is a Believer's true friend.

Have you ever wondered why Darwinists, Humanists and others spend so much time attacking Christians and biblical concepts if they do not believe they are true? It is about time.

Most people believe the age of the earth can be measured in *billions of years.* I believed that also—until I learned the information I now share with others. However, this commonly held belief is not because the scientific evidence demands such a conclusion.

Think about it. Whether people believe the earth is thousands of years old or *billions of years* old, they have the same evidence to observe. Thus, everyone's belief in the age of the earth is a matter of whose interpretation of the evidence they accept.

Because old-earth beliefs, which serve as the foundation for the religious beliefs of Darwinism, Naturalism, and Secular Humanism, are taught as if they were scientific facts today, most people think it is a scientific fact that the earth is *billions of years* old. But is such teaching an observable, testable, scientific fact?

... keep that which is committed to thy trust, avoiding profane and vain babblings, and oppositions of science falsely so called: Which some professing have erred concerning the faith. 1 Timothy 6:20-21

Real science is based on observable evidence. Observation-based science will lead to the truth, and the Truth is found in God.

However, we must be wise and discern between true science and faulty, anti-God interpretations of the world that masquerade as science. In fact, we are told to avoid such false knowledge, such false science. Take *billions of years* beliefs. No one observed long ages of time. Even human history only goes back in time a few thousand years.

Billions of years of time is a belief, not a scientific fact.

You might be thinking, so why does the age of our planet matter? It matters because it has to do with when death entered the world. Old-earth beliefs place death before mankind and this undermines people's faith in the foundations of the Gospel.

I refer to the biblical foundations, which are laid down in Genesis 1 and 3, as the **COSt**. This stands for God's perfect (**C**)reation corrupted by Adam's (**O**)riginal Sin which (**S**)eparated mankind from God (while allowing death to enter the world) requiring we be **†** (the Cross) redeemed with our loving Creator who is also our redeeming Savior, Lord Jesus the Christ.

Beliefs that place death prior to the arrival of mankind are in direct conflict with these biblical foundations. When such beliefs are presented as if they were scientific facts they cause people to place their trust in man's opinion as opposed to God's Word, leading many to reject the Lord Jesus. So, beware of "science falsely so called."

In Chapters 1 through 6 I will discuss my list of the *Top Ten Old-Earth Beliefs*. I will state the old-earth interpretations of the world we live in, include some facts that Secularists would prefer you not know, and interpret the same facts through a biblical view. For many people this information will be eternally life-changing.

Let's begin by taking a look at the Big Bang, the concept of uniformity, and starlight.

Chapter One

The Big Bang, Uniformity, and Starlight

Old-earth beliefs serve as the foundation for Darwinism; Darwinism is the foundation for modern Naturalism; and Naturalism is the foundation for Humanism. These are four religious beliefs, and if they lose "billions of years" they lose it all.

Russ Miller

The Earth formed as a result of the Big Bang.

The Big Bang is an ever-evolving theory which tries to adapt to fit with new data as it is discovered. The popular form of the Big Bang, which is not necessarily what most cosmologists believe, is that all energy and matter was once condensed into a tiny dot (called a singularity). Then, sometime between 6 billion and 20 billion years ago, the dot exploded. This is what Sir Fred Hoyle referred to as the Big Bang, and the name stuck.

Part of this belief is that about 4.6 billion years ago the earth formed as a big ball of molten rock from which all life was eventually brought forth. However, observable science often conflicts with these unobserved beliefs.

The First Law of Thermodynamics is the Law of Conservation of Mass and Energy. Simply stated, this scientific principle holds that matter or energy cannot be created or destroyed; matter can be transformed into energy, and energy can be changed into matter; however, the total amount of the two remains the same. The First Law conflicts with the secular belief that all energy and matter were confined to a tiny *singularity*.

The Second Law of Thermodynamics is the Law of Entropy. This is the most accepted of all scientific principles (except for within *evolutionary biology* which falsely teaches that things evolve into more complex life forms over *billions of years*). The Second Law holds that things wear down, lose energy, and become less organized over time. Simply put, things become worse and worse, not better and better. The Second Law conflicts with the secular beliefs that the universe began with a great explosion, then organized itself into our solar system and eventually into all the highly complex forms of life on earth today.

Logic holds that for every result which had a beginning there must be a cause which is outside of, and not a part of, the result. There can be no such thing as an "uncaused event." In other words, the cause of the universe had to have been in existence outside of the universe's space, matter, and time in order to cause the universe to come into existence.

So, according to the First and Second Laws, and logic, the universe could not have created itself and then become more and more organized over time as required by Big Bang cosmologies.

A letter signed by dozens of scientists was published in *New Scientist* during 2004. Titled *Bucking the Big Bang*, statements included:
The Big Bang theory can boast no predictions that have been validated by observation.
The Big Bang relies on a growing number of never-observed entities, inflation, dark matter, dark energy...and can't survive without these fudge factors...In no other field of physics would this continual recourse to new hypothetical factors be accepted.
Claimed successes consist of retrospectively making observations fit by adding adjustable parameters. 1

As Dr. Fred Hoyle observed: *Be suspicious of a theory if more and more hypotheses are needed to support it as new facts become available.* 2

The April 2011 cover of *Science Magazine* claimed the current Big Bang theory needs to be discarded because it has too many problems to be fixed. Yet this theory, man's knowledge, has been taught to high school and college students as if it were actually fact for the past fifty years, corrupting the faith of young minds in the Word of God.

However, the Big Bang is turning out to be a Big Dud, leaving Secularists without a viable explanation for how the universe, or the earth, came about. As a result, they continue to push ideas which have already been refuted and bend observations to fit their unobserved hypothesis.

The biblical view of how the universe and the earth came into existence is found throughout Scripture. In Exodus 20 we are given God's Ten Commandments which were etched into stone by God's own finger. Regarding the Sabbath day God told us:

11 *For in six days the LORD made heaven and earth, the sea, and all that in them is, and rested the seventh day...*

In Genesis 2 we learn that the First Law of Thermodynamics, the Law of Conservation of Mass and Energy, was most likely put into place by our Creator following the sixth day of Creation:

1-2 *Thus the heavens and the earth were finished, and all the host of them. And on the seventh day God ended his work which he had made...*

When God said His Creation activity was finished, He meant it.

The Second Law of Thermodynamics, the Law of Entropy, is likely a part of God's curse on our fallen world and is described in several verses such as Isaiah 51:6:

...for the heavens shall vanish away like smoke, and the earth shall wax old like a garment, and they that dwell therein shall die in like manner: but my salvation shall be forever, and my righteousness shall not be abolished.

God put the natural laws into place, among them the First and Second Laws of Thermodynamics. As their Creator, He can act outside of them as He chooses.

Of all ancient religious texts, only the biblical God claimed to be both eternal...

...from everlasting to everlasting, thou art God. Psalms 90:2

...and to exist outside of the universe's space, matter and time.

...I am not of the world John 17:16

These verses leave all non-Christians, and Christians who accept man's knowledge over God's knowledge and wisdom, out of step with both science and logic. Yet observable science and logic fit perfectly with our biblical Creator being the external Cause of the universe's space, matter and time. 3 The Bible, in Jeremiah 2, foretold that people would turn their back on God and claim we came from a rock:

27 *Saying...to a stone, Thou hast brought me forth: for they have turned their back unto me...*

Wow! God's Word is awesome, and there is no logical or viable scientific reason to believe that we came from a ball of rock, a stone, which was the result of a Big Bang.

As Nobel Prize-winning astrophysicist, Dr. Arno Penzias stated, " The best data we have are exactly what I would have predicted had I had nothing to go on but the five books of Moses." 4

My advice is that we place our faith in our Creator, Lord Jesus the Christ.

Uniformity: the present is the key to the past

Uniformity-based thinking is the key to the entire old-earth dating system. Unlike the old-earth beliefs of the ancient Greeks, modern day old-earth beliefs are founded upon the belief that processes observed today are basically the same as they have been since the earth began. The word for this belief is *uniformitarianism*.

While the term sounds daunting, all it means is that things have always remained fairly constant, or uniform. This is the foundation of today's old-earth beliefs. People who accept this belief think *the present is the key to the past.*

For example, people could measure the amount of silt being removed from Grand Canyon by the Colorado River today and, assuming uniformity, they could look at the size of the Canyon and believe it took the river *millions of years* to carve out the chasm. And they would be wrong (see Chapter 4). Let's use an observable example to expose the faulty concept of uniformity.

Have you ever seen a mechanic remove used oil from a car? The mechanic removes the oil pan plug, and the oil gushes into a bucket below. Then, two minutes later, the bucket is full of oil and the flow coming from the car has slowed to a gradual drip.

If people who had never seen oil drained from a car happened along at this time, and if they believed the present rate of oil dripping into the bucket had always been the same, they could very well conclude that it had taken *thousands of years* to fill that bucket with oil! But they would be wrong. 5 The demonstrable fact is that *the present is **not** the key to the unobservable past.*

The biblical view holds that the very fact the secular worldview is based on old-earth beliefs which are founded on the belief that processes observed today are basically the same as they have been since the earth began is great proof of the Spirit-led inspiration of the Bible. This is because the disciple Peter prophesied in 2 Peter 3 that in the last days scoffers would claim that all things continue as they always have since the earth began.

3-4 ***Knowing this first, that there shall come in the last days scoffers, walking after their own lusts, And saying, Where is the promise of his coming? for since the fathers fell asleep, all things continue as they were from the beginning of the creation.***

And sure enough, as foretold in the Bible, today's old-earth believers base their *billions of years* beliefs on present processes being relatively the same as past processes.

Old-earth believers assume the earth is old because they believe that the gradual strata formation observed now has continued on in relatively the same manner ever since the beginning of the world. They see the speed of light today and, thinking it has always been uniform, believe it took light *millions* or *billions of years* to get to earth: uniformity-based thinking in action as foretold in the Word of God.

I will pick up this incredible Scriptural prophecy from 2 Peter 3 as we discuss starlight later in this chapter and when I discuss the global Flood in Chapters 3 and 6. For now I will just state the simple truth: the present is not the key to the past.

Starlight takes *millions of years* to reach the earth

A light year is not a measure of time. It is a measure of distance. Light presently travels at 186,282 miles per second through earth's atmosphere. By placing their faith in uniformity, while noting the vast distances stars are located from the earth, Secularists conclude it takes starlight *millions of years* to reach our planet.

The simple truth is that had stars formed over *millions of years* and had starlight always traveled at its current speed, it surely would have taken visible starlight *millions of years* to reach our planet. So what do the facts reveal?

First, note that many star deaths have been observed while never has the birth of a new star been detected. This is yet another problem for the evolutionary view since more star births than star extinctions would be taking place if the universe were evolving.

Because of this dilemma, whenever something new is found in space that is not understood, it is often deemed to be a *star-birthing chamber.* Still, the actual scientific fact remains that never has the birth of a new star been observed.

In the meantime, researchers in labs have been able to bring light to a dead stop, capture it, and then release it. Since mankind can change the speed of light, I see no scientific reason to believe that today's speed of light has always been constant. After all, how long did it take to fill that pan with oil?

The biblical view of light is found in the first chapter of the first book in the Bible. We are told in Genesis 1 that on the first day of the Creation week, God's Spirit moved upon the face of the waters which were covering the newly formed orb:

3-5 And God said, Let there be light: and there was light. And God saw the light, that it was good: and God divided the light from the darkness. And God called the light Day, and the darkness he called Night....

In other words, God was hovering above the earth while He was making it, and during the first day He made light instantaneously at His spoken word.

Since humans can alter the speed of light, I see no reason to doubt that the Creator of light can do so as well. Thus, we can trust that God provided light exactly when and where He claims to have done so.

Skeptics have told me that a sudden change in the speed of light would disrupt the proton-to-neutron balance and instantly end all life. Though I have not looked into this claim I figure that, if true, it may explain why the Creator of all life got light here on the first day of His Creation. This was before He created life on days three, five and six. It was also prior to the natural laws which God put in place after the sixth day to govern His Creation. Interestingly, while God made light on the first day, He did not make the sun, moon and stars until the fourth day of the Creation week.

We are told in Genesis 1:14 that God made the stars to provide:

...signs, and for seasons, and for days, and years:

Note that God knows the difference between a day and a year

and God made the stars to be seen immediately for signs, and for the tracking of time which was also a part of His Creation.

An eye-opening part of the biblical view of starlight, prophesied in 2 Peter 3, is that in the latter days scoffers would claim uniformity (light has always traveled at a constant rate of speed from distant stars to planet earth) while denying that God made the heavens mature:

5 *For this they willingly are ignorant of, that by the word of God the heavens were of old...*

Today skeptics are pleading *uniformity* to claim that it takes starlight *millions of years* to reach our planet. God's Word is amazing!

Old-earthers err due to having rejected God's Word about His week-long Creation and His global judgment by water. These are two keys to the earth's history, and aside from these two events, things have been relatively uniform.

The truth is that the present is not the key to the past. Instead, God's Word is the key to the present.

"At college I'm bombarded with evolution, atheism and professors who present 'facts' against the Bible. I sought advice but no one could answer the questions. I began to accept my faith was going to die. Then I heard of you. I was skeptical you could refute the 'facts' but you opened my eyes or I would have lost my faith. THANK YOU!"

Brenda in AZ

Chapter Two

The Radiometric Dating Methods

To be ignorant...would be to throw down our weapons and to betray our uneducated brethren who have, under God, no defense but us against the intellectual attacks of the heathen.

C.S. Lewis

Radiometric dating

Radiometric, or radioisotope, dating techniques comprise one of what I refer to as the five pillars of today's old-earth beliefs.

The public perception, fueled by the secular media, schools, and scientific establishment, is that radiometric dating methods provide iron-clad proof that the world is *billions of years* old.

Here are the facts. It is an observable, thus scientific, fact that radioactive elements decay over time. The radioactive material is considered to be the parent element and, as it decays, it produces what is referred to as the daughter element. For instance, the parent element potassium-40 decays into the daughter material argon-40. It is also true that we have the equipment to accurately measure the amounts of both the parent and daughter elements in a particular rock.

Based on the known rate that a parent element presently decays into the daughter material, combined with measuring the amounts of the parent and the daughter elements in a rock, an approximate age for the rock is obtained (note: this is actually a measurement of radioactive decay, not of time). In other words the various radiometric dating techniques indicate that it took X number of years for the current amount of the daughter element to form.

There are about fifty different combinations of elements employed as methods of radioisotope dating. These include potassium-argon, potassium-calcium, samarium-neodymium, rubidium-strontium, uranium-lead, thorium-lead, and lead-lead.

Initially these dating methods sound viable. However, the observable fact is that each method requires that several guesses, referred to as assumptions, be made in order to come up with an age for the rock being dated. These unobserved guesses corrupt the validity of the ages provided by the various radioisotope dating methods.

Because of the erroneous belief that these methods are reliable, let us take a look at the isotope dating methods in action. Since potassium-argon is one of the most popular of the methods, I will use it in this discussion.

It is an observable fact that potassium-40 decays into argon-40. It is also true that we can accurately measure the amounts of the parent and daughter elements in the rock being dated.

Furthermore, today's rate of decay from potassium-40 to argon-40 has been determined by observable scientific methods. However, this is where the science comes to a halt and the assumptions take over, corrupting the integrity of the radiometric dating results. These dating techniques are used on igneous rock. This is because the *unobserved assumption* is made that the melting process which occurred when the rock formed started the radiometric clock. In other words it is assumed that none of the daughter material, argon in this example, was in the rock when the rock formed.

However, no one was there to observe whether or not the daughter element was in the rock when it first formed. Since the age given to the rock is based on how long the amount of argon in the rock took to form, if argon was present in the rock from the start, the radiometric age will be *millions* or *billions of years* older than what the rock really is.

Then there is the issue of contamination. Amounts of both the parent and the daughter materials can be added to, or lost from, a rock. Contamination can be caused by heat, pressure, moisture, earthquakes and more. To blindly assume that a rock has existed for *millions* or *billions of years* and has never been contaminated by the addition or loss of either the parent or the daughter material is anything but scientific.

The fact is that no one was there to observe whether or not contamination occurred. Since the age given to the rock sample is based on the amounts of the parent and daughter elements presently found in the rock, if any potassium or argon was added to the rock, or lost from it, the radiometric age will be off by *millions* or *billions of years.*

Still another wild guess affecting all radiometric dating results is the *unobservable belief* that the decay rates observed today for the various parent elements have always been the same—uniformity.

Yet more and more research is bringing this assumption into question. 6 And if this assumption is wrong, the age given by any of the radiometric dating methods will be off by *millions* or *billions of years.*

Two more assumptions are: there was never a worldwide Flood which laid down the earth's strata layers quickly, and God had nothing to do with anything. So these methods are biased against the Word of God before the dating process even begins. It is tragic that billions of people have lost their faith in the God of the Bible because they were fooled into thinking radiometric dating results, man's knowledge, has trumped God's Word.

Once a person realizes the number of unobserved wild guesses employed by the radiometric dating methods, that individual will understand why *supposed* science does NOT prove that the earth is millions, much less billions, of years old. Though radiometric methods may include many scientific facts, the techniques are anything but scientific!

...avoiding profane and vain babblings, and oppositions of science falsely so called: Which some professing have erred concerning the faith. 1 Timothy 6:20-21

We are told to avoid false knowledge, false science. As I often say, real science is a Believer's best friend, but we must be wise and discern between observable evidences and misguided interpretations of evidences masquerading as science.

Knowing the radiometric dating techniques rely on several unobservable assumptions, it may not surprise to you to learn that they provide a wide range of ages for any particular rock when different isotope dating methods are used to age it.

Take, for example, Cardenas Basalt lava flows found in Grand Canyon. These rocks were radioisotope dated by potassium-argon isochrones at .51 billion years old yet also dated by samarium-neodymium as being more than three times as old—1.7 billion years old! [7]

It is accurate to say that the radiometric dating methods are un-reliable, nonscientific and biased against the Word of God.

So how do those who believe the earth is *billions of years* old decide which of the ages produced by the radiometric dating methods is correct? Since these are published as if they were proven facts in school textbooks and scientific journals, we need to know!

The answer is that published radiometric dates are selected once an age is obtained that matches another old-earth dating system, the man-made Geologic Time Scale, also referred to as the Geologic Column. Rocks are dated over and over until a date is obtained that matches the Geologic Time Scale. Non-matching dates are tossed out while the matching age is *selected*.

For example, during 1972 a human skull was found in a layer of rock which had already been dated as being *230 million years* old. Well, such a fossil find certainly did not fit the Geologic Time Scale, so the age of the strata was changed from *230 million years* old to *1.8 million years* old. Secular geologists date the rock by the fossils and the fossils by the rock according to the ages assigned to the man-made Geologic Column, as I will explain in the next chapter. [8]

Occam's Razor is the principle that the simplest answer (the one that makes the fewest assumptions) is, other things being equal, generally better than more complex explanations.

The biblical view is that:
- Earth's sedimentary layers which were laid down by water formed during God's global Flood judgment of man's sin.
- radiometric dating methods are corrupted due to being based on mankind's erroneous assumptions of gradual strata formation, and
- God's wisdom trumps man's limited knowledge once again.

Occam's razor

Carbon dating is the best known of the isotope dating methods. In this dating method, the amount of Carbon-14 is measured in organic remains, that is, in the remains of plants or animals.

C-14 is produced in the earth's atmosphere when cosmic rays enter the atmosphere and create fast-moving neutrons. These neutrons collide with Nitrogen-14 atoms and change the N-14 into radioactive C-14 atoms.[9] Trace amounts of C-14 exist in plants and animals because during the process of photosynthesis, plants take in CO_2, which contains tiny amounts of C-14. Meanwhile, animals ingest C-14 when they eat or breathe. However, once a plant or animal dies it stops taking in C-14 which gradually decays back into N-14.

Because today's rate of decay has been established and since we have the instruments to accurately measure the amount of C-14 and N-14 in an organic remain, simply stated, the less C-14 in the remain, the older it will be aged by the carbon dating method (note: this is a measurement of radioactive decay, not of time).

Up to this point, the process sounds fairly straightforward. Unfortunately, just as with the radiometric dating methods which are used on igneous rock, this is where the real science comes to an end as *unobserved assumptions* corrupt the integrity of carbon dating results.

For example, technicians have to assume that the organic remains being tested lay in the ground for long periods of time yet were never contaminated by the gain or loss of C-14. Yet moisture, heat, pressure and other conditions can each cause contamination.

Since the age given to the organic material is based on how much C-14 is found in the item being dated, not knowing how much contamination occurred corrupts the integrity of the carbon dating procedure.

Other carbon dating assumptions include the notion that today's rates of atmospheric production and decay have always been the same—uniformity. However, no one was there to observe this, and if either guess is wrong, all carbon dating results are completely inaccurate and observable facts strongly suggest the present is not the key to the past.

For example, earth's magnetic field is known to have weakened by more than 6% since the 1850s. This means that the magnetic field used to be stronger than it is today. A stronger field would have blocked a lot of the cosmic rays from entering the atmosphere, reducing the production and the amount of C-14 in the world. As a result, plants and animals living in the past ingested less C-14 than do their descendants that live today. This means creatures living 800 years ago would have had a lower percentage of C-14 in them when they died than plants or animals that lived 400 years ago, and much lower than ones that lived just 100 years ago. The net result is a multiplying effect on assigned ages. In other words, things living in the past will carbon date substantially older than they really are.

Yet again we see that *the present is not the key to the past.*

As of this writing, the few scientists who actually operate carbon dating equipment seem to agree that measurable amounts of C-14 should decay away, at today's rate, in 40,000 to 100,000 years. To be as fair as possible, I will go with the 100,000 year timeframe.

This means the oldest age carbon dating could provide would be 100,000 years, since measurable amounts of C-14 would be gone beyond that amount of time. Yet C-14 has been discovered in diamonds, oil, natural gas, coal and other organic samples which Secularists tell us are *millions* or *billions of years* old. [10]

Even more revealing is that the Cambrian layer, the lowest strata layer containing appreciable amounts of fossils, which secular geologists claim is about 570,000,000 years old, still contains measurable amounts of C-14. This means that the Cambrian layer is less than 100,000 years old! [11]

Even more astounding is that scientific tests have found that all strata layers not only contain C-14, but in the same range of amounts from the top strata all the way down through the Cambrian layer! Since C-14 decays away over time, this discovery strongly indicates all of these layers formed during the same event! [12]

To explain the existence of C-14 in material that, according to the Geologic Time Scale, is millions or billions of years old, old-earthers claim the materials were contaminated with the C-14 found in them today. This is an incredulous claim in light of the fact that all secular biased radiometric dating results depend on the assumption that contamination never occurred!

Many researchers claim carbon dating is fairly accurate when used on organic remains that are less than 2,500 years old. However, I suggest this is because they can calibrate dates to fit with known historical events.

Take for example a cotton vest which is known to have come from a civilization that wore the vest 1,800 to 1,900 years ago. Guess what the carbon dating age is going to be? About 1,850 years old.

Time and again the assumptions employed in the various radiometric dating procedures are shown to be inaccurate.

Yet, due to the secular control of the media, scientific and educational establishments, the public is kept in the dark about the unreliability of these faulty dating techniques. As a result, most people think they are accurate when, in fact, nothing could be further from the truth.

It is vital to understand that the Geologic Time Scale is where the ages actually come from because once you understand how these dating methods fit together and how old-earth ages are derived, you will realize that God's uncompromised Word trumps mankind's limited knowledge.

I will cover the Geologic Column dating system further in the next chapter.

The biblical view is that the global Flood laid down the earth's sedimentary layers of rock, including all the things those layers contain, just a few thousand years ago during the global Flood. Thus, we should find C-14 in the same range of amounts throughout the water-borne sediments, and this is exactly what is found! Carbon dating provides great support for the biblical worldview.

The biblical view includes the idea that the radioisotope dating methods are based on mankind's fallible interpretations of the earth, and that God's wisdom trumps man's limited knowledge yet again.

Occam's razor

"We had a lot of questions and you answered every question we had and more! I am so excited!"

Julia in WA

Chapter Three

No Global Flood and the Geologic Column

Old-earthers will deny the global Flood to their death because such a Flood destroys death before Adam, old-earth beliefs by explaining how earth's strata layers formed quickly.

Russ Miller

In this chapter I will discuss two more of what I refer to as the five pillars of old-earth beliefs: **there was never a global Flood**, and the **Geologic Column**. These two go hand-in-hand.

There has never been a global Flood

Until the mid-1800s, most people believed the earth was a few thousand years old. They accepted that our planet had been judged with a global Flood that had laid down the sedimentary layers of rock which comprise the outer crust of the earth.

As it is important to have a frame of reference in order to conduct scientific investigation of our planet, scientists in the early 1800s, including several Christians, developed the **Geologic Column.**

Unfortunately, it did not take long for old-earth beliefs, founded on a belief in *uniformity*, to corrupt the observable science behind the Column.

Secularists, who placed their faith in uniformity, correctly observed that present rates of strata formation were extremely slow. They then erroneously assumed that the unobservable past rates of strata accumulation were gradual as well. Then, by denying the earth had endured a global Flood, they determined it had taken *millions of years* for earth's strata layers to form.

Based on these non-observed beliefs, the Geologic Column was quickly turned into a time scale that replaced the global Flood, fooled billions of people into accepting *death before Adam* beliefs, and undermined billions of people's faith in God's Word.

The Geologic Column, also known as the Geologic Time Scale, is a drawing consisting of twelve primary layers. Each layer was given a name, assigned index fossils, and given an ancient age. Charles Lyell popularized the Geologic Column in his book *The Principles of Geology* which was published in 1830.

Since this system for dating the earth was invented when state-of-the-art weaponry was a musket and when modern transportation was a horse-drawn carriage, a fair question is how did these individuals derive the ages they assigned to the rock layers? There is only one viable response: They made up the ages of the rock layers based on their belief that the layers had formed gradually at the same pace as they could observe at that time— uniformity.

Note:
Keep in mind that the Geologic Column is where radiometric ages are selected from. A worldwide Flood explains how earth's strata layers formed quickly, destroying old-earth beliefs. This is why old-earth believers deny the global Flood and/or the evidence of it.

Index fossils are an integral part of the Geologic Time Scale, or Column. Index fossils are fossils of plants and animals which were assumed to have gone extinct while a particular layer of rock was gradually forming. Having supposedly gone extinct during that particular period of strata formation, their remains would not be found in younger layers lying above the fossil's extinction layer. Thus, whenever an index fossil is found, everything in the layer containing the remains is given the age that the inventors of the Column assigned to that specific fossil. In other words, the ages of rock layers are derived from the index fossils found in them while the ages of the index fossils are obtained from which rock layer they are found in.

This is circular reasoning at its finest.

Another fair question is how did the inventors of the Geologic

Column know which plants and animals had become extinct during the unobserved formation of the various strata layers?

Obviously they could not have known and today, the much-heralded index fossils of the Geologic Column, on which the old-earth beliefs have been built, have turned into a stupendous embarrassment to the old-earth faithful as they keep showing up alive! In fact, they are being found alive by the dozens.

So many supposedly *extinct* plants and animals are being found alive today that a scientific classification has been made for them. No, I am not kidding. They are referred to as Lazarus Taxon because they have seemingly risen from the dead! However, they never were extinct and Lazarus Taxon undermines the very basis of the Geologic Time Scale. Think about it. The layers of the Geologic Column have been assigned vast ages based on many unobserved beliefs including how long some plants and animals have been extinct. Now we know that many were not extinct and, in fact, are still alive today.

This invalidates the Geologic Time Scale, from which radiometric ages are selected. And Lazarus Taxon are not the worst news that real, observation-based science has for unobserved *billions of years* beliefs.

If the earth's stratified rock layers did indeed form gradually over *billions of years*, how much of the earth's crust should we expect to be comprised of the twelve primary layers of the Geologic Column, in the correct order, with the corresponding index fossils by which the layers are identified? 100%? 75%? 50%? 25%?

Had the layers formed slowly over long ages of time I would expect the Column to exist in at least 50%, if not 90%, of our planet's crust. What would you think?

Despite what you or I might expect, according to the old-earth faithful, the vaunted Geologic Column only exists in about .5% of the earth's crust. That is, even the researchers who place their faith in this old-earth dating system admit that it is not found in 99.5% of the earth's surface! And to my knowledge the scant .5% of the earth's surface which is claimed to hold the Geologic Column does not contain the proper order of the infamous index fossils. Thus the question becomes: Does the Column exist at all in the natural world? I must say that, as of this writing, I have not been convinced that it does.

And the Geologic Time Scale is where modern-day old-earth beliefs were derived. It is where the published radiometric dates are selected. What does this tell you about *death before Adam*, old-earth beliefs?

Please consider: Only radiometric ages that match the Column are published. Next, since they match each other, the claim is made that this proves both types of old-earth dating methods work. And the world, including many Christians, has been taken in by this false science.

Ever-growing numbers of scientific discoveries are revealing that *the present is NOT the key to the past*. Many times the rapid formation of strata layers, canyons and other geological processes have been observed during catastrophic events.

In fact, studies show that it takes a cataclysmic event to stratify layers.

Whenever large mixtures of various-sized grains are moved by volcanic activity or massive water flow, they can rapidly segregate into stratified layers by grain size and density. Larger grains tend to be found at the base of the strata while smaller grains usually end up on the top.

The May 18, 1980 eruption of Mount St. Helens in Washington State, along with its aftermath, provided some of the most scientifically-observed geological processes in all of history.

These observed events revealed three different ways strata layers can form quickly.

1. A twenty-five-foot-thick layer of strata was laid down in a matter of minutes by flows that rushed from the volcano's crater at over 200 miles per hour.
2. Air-fall deposits formed finely stratified layers in a matter of days following the eruption as debris fell back to earth. In fact, in some locations several hundred feet of finely stratified strata layers were laid down in a matter of minutes.
3. On March 19, 1982, surging water and mud flows carved a canyon through these layers. This event also laid down a finely stratified layer on top of the previously deposited layers. And all formed rapidly, not over never observed *millions* or *billions of years* of time.

However, if Humanists lose their foundation of long ages of time, they lose everything. So despite these scientifically observed events, unobserved old-earth interpretations of canyon and strata formation continue to be taught in schools. That is secular indoctrination as opposed to scientific education.

Mudstones

A key to old-earth beliefs is the notion that earth's sedimentary layers of rock, which make up about 78% of the outer crust of the earth, were NOT laid down during a global Flood.

Secular geologists have been using mudstones, which make up about 67% of earth's strata layers, as one of their primary evidences against the global Flood. Old-earthers have been claiming that swift water currents, such as the planet would have endured during a worldwide Flood, would have disrupted any previously deposited layers.

Based on this unobserved, erroneous assumption, secular geology has been teaching that clay particles settled gradually and uniformly to the floor of calm bodies of water over long ages of time to form the mudstones. Again we see assumptions based upon assumptions being passed off as if they were scientific facts.

However, during 2007, these old-earth beliefs were refuted by real science. Researchers at Indiana University ran a series of experiments which allowed them to observe the accumulation of mudstone strata. Testing various types of mud in both salt and fresh water flows revealed that mudstone layers can form in either tranquil seas or in swift-moving waters.

The biblical view, found in Genesis, the first book of the Bible, is that God's original Creation was *very good* until Adam's original sin corrupted it. Then, due to man's continuing sinfulness, God destroyed His Creation via a global Flood approximately 4,500 years ago.

Genesis 7:19-20 ***And the waters prevailed exceedingly upon the earth; and all the high hills, that were under the whole heaven, were covered. Fifteen cubits upward did the waters prevail; and the mountains were covered.***

The aftermath of a Flood in which *all the high hills that were under the whole heaven were covered* should be significant. For example, I would expect that the outer crust of the earth we can observe today would primarily consist of sedimentary layers of rock that were deposited by water. I would also expect to find significant lava flows interspersed among the sedimentary layers.

I would further predict that the strata layers would contain the fossils of plants and creatures that had been drowned and buried so quickly that they did not have time to rot away or be eaten by bacteria, worms, or other scavengers.

And what do we observe today? The outer crust of the earth we now live on averages a mile deep of sedimentary layers of rock that were deposited by water. These layers are interspersed with lava flows, and the strata layers contain billions of fossils of plants and creatures that were buried so quickly that they did not have time to rot away or be eaten by scavengers.

Occam's razor

Secular textbooks teach that **fossils and petrified logs** found in the rock layers formed over *millions of years*. However, no one has ever witnessed anything taking place over long ages of time, while many examples of rapid fossilization and petrification have been observed. Fence posts, hats, water wheels and more have been found which are known to have turned to stone in fewer than seventy years.

The fact is that for a plant or animal to become a fossil it must be rapidly buried before bacteria, worms, insects or animals can eat it or before oxygen or chemicals can cause it to decay away. Once buried, minerals, such as calcite (calcium carbonate) and silica (silicon dioxide) that have been dissolved and transported by groundwater, gradually replace bone, tooth and plant material. This leaves behind a fossil shaped like the bone, tooth or plant the minerals replaced.[13]

However, if Humanists lose long ages of time, they lose everything. So despite these observable scientific discoveries, secular schools, colleges and textbooks continue to deny the global Flood while teaching unsuspecting students the dubious old-earth interpretations of the world that have been taught for the past century. Is it any wonder that the majority of geologists believe the earth is *billions of years* old and that there was never a global Flood? It is not because the evidence demands it. It is because old-earth interpretations are all they have been taught. In the meantime, the testable, observable facts support the Word of God.

Another part of the biblical worldview regarding the worldwide deluge is a most revealing proof that the Bible is the inspired word of our Creator, Judge and redeeming Savior, Lord Jesus the Christ. This is the continuing prophecy about end time scoffers found in 2 Peter 3:5-6

For this they willingly are ignorant of...Whereby the world that then was, being overflowed with water, perished:

Absolutely astounding! 1,900 years ago the Word of God foretold that doubters would deny the global Flood in the latter days, and this is EXACTLY what old-earth believers do today. Amazing!

So why would someone deny the worldwide deluge? The answer is simple. Such an event would erode old-earth beliefs which are based upon the belief that earth's strata layers formed gradually and uniformly over long ages of unobserved time. A global Flood explains how earth's sedimentary layers of rock, which were laid down by water, formed quickly.

Thus a worldwide Flood destroys *death before Adam* beliefs. Because of this simple truth, old-earthers deny the global Flood or its effects. In fact, they will deny God's worldwide judgment with fury if challenged because if they lose *billions of years* they lose it all.

Old-earthers err due to having rejected God's Word about His week-long Creation and His year-long global judgment by water. These are two keys to the earth's real history, and aside from these two events, things have been relatively uniform.

A visualization of the global Flood will explain many of earth's geological features through a biblical view in Chapter 20.

When it comes to the age of the earth, the truth is that the present has never been the key to the past. Instead, God's Word is the key to the past and the global Flood is the key to understanding the age of the earth.

"I hold an advanced degree in geology. Your presentation on the global flood has been a real eye-opener! Thank you very much."
Don in AZ

"Russ, I'm a geologist and I want to commend you on your excellent materials!"
Brent in MT

Chapter Four

Grand Canyon and the Grand Staircase

Old-Earth beliefs are the substance of years imagined, the evidence of time unobserved.

Russ Miller

Grand Canyon

Grand Canyon is another of the five pillars of old-earth beliefs. More than 900 cubic miles of sediment have been removed to form Grand Canyon in Northern Arizona. By measuring the amount of sediment presently being carried out of the chasm by the Colorado River, and assuming that the present rates are the same as past rates of erosion (uniformity), secular scientists concluded it took *millions of years* for the river to form Grand Canyon. However, the two most popular old-earth interpretations of how Grand Canyon formed have been scientifically debunked, and have been for a number of years!

A major hurdle for the belief that the Colorado River carved out the Canyon is that the river enters Grand Canyon about a mile below the top rim of the gorge... and water doesn't flow uphill.

In order to explain how the river eroded the canyon, uniformity-minded researchers came up with the Ancient River Theory, also known as the Antecedent River Theory. This hypothesis holds that the water flow was eroding the chasm at the exact same rate at which the Kaibab Upwarp, through which the canyon slices, was uniformly and slowly uplifting over *millions of years*. Talk about a miracle! Though taught as fact for nearly a century, the Ancient River Theory has been thoroughly refuted from a scientific standpoint and has been for fifty years.

One of many problems for this idea is the Wasatch layers which were deposited against the side of the already-formed Kaibab Upwarp. The order that the two events occurred can be discerned as the Wasatch layers were not uplifted along with the strata layers of the Kaibab Upwarp, against which the Wasatch layers lie. This attests to the fact they were laid down after the uplifting took place.

However, the event which knifed through the Upwarp to form Grand Canyon cut through both the uplifted strata as well as through the horizontal Wasatch layers. This proves that the Kaibab Upwarp formed first, the Wasatch layers were laid down afterward, and the event that eroded Grand Canyon occurred last. Like I often say, real science is a Believer's best friend. Rarely do I hear anyone touting the Ancient River Theory today, though untold millions of people have been misled because of it.

Next came the Stream Capture, or Precocious Gulley Theory. This is more of an excuse than a viable theory. After all, Grand Canyon is one of the five pillars of old-earth beliefs, so those who worship at the altar of old-earth beliefs cannot afford to admit the gorge formed quickly. Though this tale is currently the primary old-earth excuse for the formation of Grand Canyon, it is rather far-fetched to say the least.

This tale holds that the Colorado River was slowly eroding the chasm from one direction while rain runoff was gradually eroding a gully on the other side of the Upwarp. Eventually the two canyons met at Kanab Creek where they joined up to form Grand Canyon. Having led river-rafting trips through Grand Canyon, I can attest firsthand to the utter impossibility of this tale.

First, the site where the two erosion events supposedly met is along a spectacular two-mile straight stretch of the gorge where the rock walls tower 700+ feet straight up from the river's edge. The steep walls are solid proof that the chasm was carved out quickly via massive water flow, not gradually over *millions of years*. Also, Kanab Creek turns away from the 700-foot tall cliffs at a 90-degree angle and immediately turns into the meandering loops of a slow-moving stream. This is not indicative of the type of flow required to have formed the 700-foot tall canyon walls.

The towering walls of the gorge match up perfectly where the two unobserved erosion events were supposed to have come together. There is no spot where one can say, "Here is where two separate gullies came together." This strongly implies that such an event never took place. The observable evidence reveals that the Stream Capture Theory is simply wishful thinking by those not wanting to admit Grand Canyon formed quickly.

If you have not previously heard this information, it is because Secularists do not have a viable way to explain how Grand Canyon could have formed slowly over long ages of time, so they suppress the evidence against its gradual formation and continue to allude to the debunked Stream Capture hypothesis.

If you've ever visited Grand Canyon National Park, you know exactly what I mean. You likely read the old-earth propaganda in the literature they give to you upon entering the park. You probably saw the signs at the viewpoints, heard a park ranger rattle on about *millions of years*, or hiked along the rim trail's *Geologic Trail of Time*, complete with bronze medallions and cement pedestals showcasing rocks and *billions of years* of time.

Due to the faulty misinterpretations of Grand Canyon pushed by the secular park service and secular schools, Grand Canyon has been used to fool billions of people into doubting or denying God's Word.

Let's discuss the strata layers through which Grand Canyon slices as well as the area around Grand Canyon. You will see that the geological formations in the region around the Canyon provide great support of the global Flood which destroys *billions of years*, *death before Adam*, beliefs.

The stratified layers of the Kaibab Upwarp through which Grand Canyon cuts are sedimentary layers that were laid down by water. Marine fossils such as sea lily stems, sponges, scallops, clams and brachiopods are found in these layers.

There are no *time gaps* between the rock layers. For example, had a strata layer laid on the surface for *millions of years* before the layer above it formed, evidence should include water erosion, plant growth and acids leaching from the ancient rocks on the surface of the lower layer. These would be *time gaps*. However, the *time gaps* are not there, revealing that the layers did not form gradually over *billions of years*.

Then there are the squished Polonium halos. Allow me to explain. Polonium-210 emits energy for about two years after it forms. The energy forms colored circles around the element and, if caught in a log that petrifies or a rock that hardens during that two-year period, produces what are called radio halos. Circular halos that got squished into an elongated shape when the layer above them was deposited are found in the Jurassic, Triassic, and Eocene layers of the Colorado plateau.

However, after being squished, the circular pattern began forming again. This proves these layers, supposedly representing 250 million years on the Geologic Time Scale, actually formed within months of each other, while the energy was still being emitted from the Polonium! [14]

Another major embarrassment to the believers in uniformity is the missing strata layers in Grand Canyon. These are referred to as *unconformities*. The standard old-earth, *death before Adam* line is that the missing layers, some of which represent up to 1.2 billion years of missing strata, were somehow eroded before the existing layer above was deposited...but NOT by a worldwide Flood! And there are several unconformities found between Grand Canyon layers.

The biblical view is that the Flood waters stratified the layers quickly, leaving no *time gaps* between them. The surging waters were laying down layers and picking them up again throughout the year-long deluge. As the waters sloshed back and forth after the mountains arose and the valleys sank down toward the end of the Flood, some layers were removed and others were buried as unconformities by late Flood sediment deposits.

After the layers formed, through which Grand Canyon eventually cut, a major fault occurred below the surface of the ground. As a result, the strata were lifted up about 4,000 feet to form the Kaibab Upwarp. Interestingly, the bent rock is not cracked into a trillion pieces as should be expected had the layers been rock at the time of the event.

Many examples of folded yet unbroken strata layers are found within the Canyon's walls as well. Folded strata in Carbon Creek and 75-Mile Creek are great examples that I show people when I lead biblically-based river rafting adventures.

The biblical view is that strata layers are bent, yet the rock isn't broken because at the end of the global Flood the layers were still moist sediments freshly deposited by the Flood waters. When the *mountains arose and the valleys sank down* toward the end of the Flood, separating or smashing the earth's plates together around the globe, the event likely formed the Kaibab Upwarp. These uplifted layers have since hardened into the bent yet unbroken rock strata that we can observe today at Grand Canyon.

The sedimentary layers that were laid down by water, through which an erosion event knifed to form the red, pink and white walls of Grand Canyon, are a testament to God's global judgment by water and to the Truth of the Bible.

Occam's razor

The second-best proof in the world of the global Flood.

Allow me to introduce you to the second-best evidence of the global Flood found anywhere in the world.

I give an *on the rim* talk during our Grand Canyon rim tours. As we stand on the Kaibab limestone which makes up the rim of the gorge, I tell folks, "If you're looking down into the Canyon and you would like to see some of the best proof of the Truth of God's Word anywhere in the world, then you're looking the wrong way!" This is because the best evidence of the global Flood, which erodes old-earth beliefs, is not found in Grand Canyon.

It is found above the Canyon's rim.

Cedar Mountain and Red Butte tower 900 feet above the Kaibab limestone. These buttes consist of the 6 0 0 -foot thick Moenkopi layer and 300-foot thick Chinle formation. Both layers were laid down by water and formerly covered the entire region, yet have been removed for thousands of square miles. We know this because the layers pick up again further north in Arizona and southern Utah, as well as east into the Painted Desert.

Think about this for a moment. While Grand Canyon represents 900+ cubic miles of missing sediments, these missing layers represent thousands of cubic miles of missing materials.

Once the people on our tours realize that these layers formerly existed on top of where they are standing, I then ask them, "How can a 900-foot thick layer of strata be removed for thousands of square miles yet leave no trace of where the displaced sediments are?"

The only logical response is that the missing strata were removed and widely dispersed the last time the global Flood waters rushed off of the region we now call the Colorado Plateau.

So how does the National Park Service explain Cedar Mountain and Red Butte? Well, their first line of defense is to ignore the scientifically observable evidence as it destroys the *billions of years* foundation for their worldview. Since 99.99% of visitors do not know anything about the buttes, silence is all that is needed to conceal the truth. If pressed for an explanation of Cedar Mountain and Red Butte, the park's fallback position has been to claim the two formations are volcanic uplifts. This is in spite of the fact they consist of stratified layers laid down by water! Realize, most park rangers and geologists are only repeating the secular interpretations of the evidence that they have been taught.

Beware of science falsely so called.

The best proof in the world of the global Flood

Now let me introduce you to the best evidence of the global Flood found anywhere on earth.

As stupendous as the missing 900 feet of strata are, they pale in comparison to the 5,000+ feet of strata layers that are missing from on top of them! That's right! There used to be sedimentary strata layers 5,000+ feet deep on top of the 900-foot thickness of rock layers that make up Cedar Mountain and Red Butte. In total, **strata layers more than a mile thick have been removed from above the rim of Grand Canyon** and these missing layers represent about 130,000 square miles of missing sediments... astounding proof of the worldwide Flood.

In case you are wondering how we know the layers once covered the area, it is because the strata layers pick up again in northern Arizona and southern Utah in what is known as the Grand Staircase.

The primary steps of the Grand Staircase are seen at the Vermillion Cliffs, Zion and Bryce Canyon. Bryce Canyon, which is a large sapping structure, rather than a canyon, is where the erosion event ended. A sapping structure forms when water suddenly rushes away from an area, causing the area to collapse downward. From Bryce south the layers have been removed in a stair step pattern known geologically as the Grand Staircase.

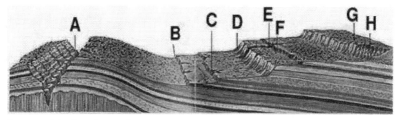

Grand Canyon (A), Chocolate Cliffs (B), Vermilion Cliffs (C), White Cliffs (D), Zion Canyon (E), Gray Cliffs (F), Pink Cliffs (G), Bryce Canyon (H). National Park Service image: public domain.

This is mind-boggling support of the global Flood, since the only logical interpretation of the removal of a mile-deep thickness of strata over such a vast region is that the layers were removed the last time the waters of the global deluge rushed off the continent at the end of the worldwide Flood.

Because the global Flood erodes *billions of years* beliefs, which provide the foundation for Darwinism, Naturalism and Humanism, and as Secularists own the park system and the educational establishments, these observable facts are glossed over or kept out of geology courses and books. False secular teachings have undermined scientific education and research as well as the eternal salvation of billions of unsuspecting people.

This is why I have developed and lead Scripturally-based Grand Canyon Rim and Grand Staircase tours. The biblical view continually provides the best interpretation of the earth because God's Word is true, word for word and cover to cover.

The Six-Day Formation of Grand Canyon

Okay, no one observed just how many days it took the waters that were ripping through the Kaibab Upwarp to carve Grand Canyon, but that's my title and I am sticking with it.

The evidence supports the gorge's rapid formation. However, whether the main canyon was completed in six days or twenty days cannot be stated dogmatically since no one was there to observe the event. I cover what I call the *Six-Day Formation of Grand Canyon* in much more detail in our DVD and PowerPoint teachings that go by this title.

Two young Christian filmmakers, Geno and Dominic DiMaria of *Block One Studios*, filmed me at the Canyon during 2010. The DVD they put together, titled *Grand Canyon*, did very well during the 2010 *San Antonio Independent Christian Film Festival*. Their production finished as a finalist in the *Young Filmmakers* category and as a semi-finalist in the *Documentary* category.

I am often asked when I present The Six-Day Formation of Grand Canyon, "If there really was a global Flood, then why don't we find hundreds of Grand Canyons around the globe?" This is a fair question which deserves a fair answer.

My response is to ask, "If the earth is really billions of years old, and if rivers carve out canyons over millions of years of time, then why don't we have millions of Grand Canyons around the world today?"

Then I employ some viable theories to explain that it took a very special set of circumstances to form Grand Canyon. Toward the end of the global Flood the thinner crusts of the earth, which had been above the fountains of the deep in the original Creation, were now underneath the heavy waters which had erupted during the first 150 days of the global deluge. Toward the latter stages of the Flood these thinner plates collapsed into the nearly empty chambers below them. This cataclysmic event created today's ocean basins while vaulting mountains skyward as the land masses shifted violently apart along the fissures left from where the fountains of the deep had been spewing forth.

As sections of land halted, often quite suddenly, geologic compression events formed. Faults occurred as well, folding the still soft layers of mud which later hardened into the folded rock layers we can observe today. The Kaibab Upwarp formed during this timeframe due to a massive fault that occurred below it.

There are several viable options as to how the Canyon formed at this point. One holds that the retreating flood waters removed the missing mile of strata, leaving behind the Grand Staircase, just prior to the formation of the Kaibab Upwarp. Then the Upwarp acted as a huge earthen dam that trapped some of the late floodwaters. After the Flood ended, the dam collected runoff from the Colorado Plateau for as much as 900 years before the waters it held breached the Upwarp and cascaded through, eroding Grand Canyon in a matter of days.

Another possibility is that the retreating Flood waters removed the missing mile of strata from the Grand Staircase region and as the waters began to dissipate, a water channel formed which carved Grand Canyon through the Kaibab Upwarp at the very end of the global Flood. Both fit the evidences well and ongoing research is trying to determine which option is most likely to have occurred.

The geological formations in and around the Canyon provide some of the best supporting proofs found anywhere in the world of the *death before Adam* destroying global Flood. For example, another one of the many problems for the old-earth interpretations of Grand Canyon is the lack of rock debris found in the chasm.

This is easy to point out when standing on the rim of Grand Canyon. As you peer down along the miles of steep, straight up and down canyon walls, it becomes very obvious that, had the Canyon formed long ago, eroding and collapsing sidewalls should have littered the Canyon floor with huge piles of boulders and rock debris.[15] However, the walls are still straight up and down for hundreds of feet and very little debris is found in the bottom of Grand Canyon. The steep rock walls are indicative of rapid formation of the abyss. The lack of rock debris reveals those walls have not stood in place for unobserved *millions of years* of time.

As of today, there is not even a viable theory to explain how Grand Canyon could have formed slowly and uniformly. That is why a growing number of secular geologists are beginning to concede that Grand Canyon formed quickly. For instance, *National Geographic for Kids* wrote, "Geologists now think that Grand Canyon grew in quick spurts from massive flooding..."[16]

An honest examination of Grand Canyon and the Grand Staircase provides great support for the biblical worldview that the global Flood is the key to the earth's geologic past and to understanding the age of our planet.

"Our trip to Grand Canyon with you was fantastic. The best part was how you brought the geology and scientific facts back to the Word of God."

Thornton and Ruth in NM

10 AM: *"Russ, my mother got me to come on your bus trip but I'm an avowed Atheist and I have no interest in your god."*
5 PM: *"Russ, this day has changed my life. Now I know that Darwinism is a lie and the Bible is true!"*

Dan in AZ

My trip to Grand Canyon with Russ was my fourth time there but having Russ explain and interpret the chasm through a biblical view, made it better than all the other trips combined."

Don in NH

Chapter Five

Dinosaurs

Dinosaurs stir the imaginations of children and adults around the world. Because most people only hear the secular interpretation of these awesome beasts, they have been used to undermine billions of people's faith in the biblical message.

Russ Miller

Dinosaur fossils were not recognized for what they were until the 1820s after Mary Mantell found a tooth that was eventually determined to be from what we now call an Iguanodon. [17]

Dr. Richard Owen created the word *dinosaur* (*deino* means terrible; *saurus* means lizard) in 1840. [18]

Dinosaurs are another of the five pillars of old-earth beliefs. Darwinists believe the *terrible lizards* evolved from a bacteria cell then went extinct about 65 *million years* ago.

As is the case with most *death before Adam* beliefs, the 65 *million years* is derived from the Geologic Column, or Time Scale, which is based upon the belief that the layers of rock in which dinosaur remains are found formed gradually and uniformly over long ages of time. If the secular view is correct, then there should be absolutely no evidence whatsoever that humans and dinosaurs lived at the same time.

In fact, Dr. Philip Kitcher wrote that if evidence showing that man and dinosaurs lived at the same time were found, it would, *"...shake the foundations of evolutionary theory."* [19]

So what does the observable evidence show?

First, realize that prior to the invention of the word dinosaur, these awesome beasts were referred to as dragons or serpents. [20] Many historical writings from 750 to 2,500 years ago contain accounts of man and dragons. We call these *dragon stories* today.

The descriptions of the beasts often sound like dinosaurs.

Alexander the Great, Apollonius of Tyana, Pliny the Elder and Marco Polo are four of the examples I use in my message, *Noah's Ark and Dinosaurs*. These historical figures wrote of dragons they were aware of in what is now India or China.[21]

Thousands of manmade designs depicting dinosaurs, which we are told are up to 2,750 years old, have been discovered around the world. These include likenesses made of bronze, wood and stone. Also, cave drawings, hieroglyphs, and petroglyphs are found around the globe, proving people had to have seen them.

Again, if the secular view were correct and dinosaurs had been extinct for 60+ *million years* before mankind came along, then there should be zero evidence that humans and dinosaurs lived during the same time. Because of this fact, any evidence showing that man and dinosaurs lived at the same time is suppressed by our secular media and schools, as such facts, *"...shake the foundations of evolutionary theory."*

And the evidence that man and dinosaurs lived at the same time is overwhelming. Other evidence that is rattling the various old-earth beliefs includes the numerous non-fossilized dinosaur bones that have been found. But even more earth-shaking for old-earth believers is that many dinosaur remains have been found that still contain biological materials such as DNA, amino acids, hemoglobin, red blood cells and pliable tissues. [22] Recent testing has also revealed that C-14 still exists in the soft tissue of a masosaur bone. Secularists claim these ocean-dwelling creatures went extinct along with the dinosaurs.

Honest scientists admit that such biological material couldn't have lasted more than a few thousand years under the best of conditions. As a result, Secularists undermine real science and scientific research by suppressing the observable evidence in order to protect their faltering religious belief. Keep in mind that if they lose long ages of time, they lose it all.

As Jesus warned in Matthew 24:4,

...Take heed that no man deceive you.

The biblical view of dinosaurs is that God made man and beast on the sixth day of the Creation week. Then, during His global judgment of man's sin, dinosaurs not on Noah's ark were drowned and buried in sedimentary layers laid down by water to form the dinosaur remains we can observe today.

I am often asked why the word *dinosaur* is not found in the Bible. The answer is that the word *dinosaur* was not invented until 1840, long after the Bible was penned by men who were inspired by the Holy Spirit. However, the words *dragon* and *serpent* are mentioned in the Scriptures more than twenty times. I believe God is discussing a large sauropod dinosaur in Job 40 when He says to Job:

15 *Behold now behemoth, which I made with thee; he eateth grass as an ox.*

The biblical view of dinosaurs, that God made man, behemoth and the other kinds of dinosaurs on the sixth day, means we once lived at the same time. Continuing with Job 40 we are told:

16-17 *...his strength is in his loins, and his force is in the navel of his belly. He moveth his tail like a cedar...*

A huge sauropod would have had tremendous strength in its mid-section so it could control its long neck and heavy head, as well as its huge tail that God compared to a cedar tree.

19 *He is the chief of the ways of God...*

The chief of the ways of God indicates this animal was one of the largest of God's creatures. Sauropods such as Apatosaurus, Diplodocus, Brachiosaurus, Supersaurus and Ultrasaurus are the largest known land animals that ever lived. They each had a tail that was comparable to a cedar tree.

Ultrasaurus has been estimated to have been 110 feet long, 60 feet tall and 150 tons in weight.[23] Perhaps Ultrasaurus was behemoth, the *chief of the ways of God.*

The biblical view holds that following Adam's original sin, (which allowed death and suffering to enter God's perfect Creation, while separating man from God), several kinds of dinosaurs did become terrible meat-eating lizards.

Around 1,650 years after the week of Creation, God judged mankind's ever-worsening sin with a worldwide deluge of water. A pair of each of the fifty or so kinds of dinosaurs, whose average size was that of a small pony, was taken aboard Noah's ark.

During the year-long Flood, the dragons not aboard the ark were drowned and buried in sedimentary layers that were laid down by water, which is where we find their remains today.

This is why dinosaur fossils abruptly appear and then suddenly disappear in the fossil record with nothing to indicate that they evolved from a bacteria cell, or anything else, into the terrible lizards that fascinate folks today.

An honest examination of observable evidences shows that dinosaurs provide great support for the biblical worldview.

"My eleven year old son watched your 'Noah's Ark & Dinosaurs' DVD. As you explained how everyone had had a chance to walk up the narrow plank way and enter God's plan of salvation from the Flood, just as we have the chance to walk up the narrow pathway into God's plan of salvation from His coming judgment, my son looked at me with tears in his eyes and said, 'I want to be saved.' We prayed right then. We watched your DVD as he likes dinosaurs but your words showed a child the way to salvation."

Stella in TX

Chapter Six

Plate Tectonics, Continental Drift, Mountains, Geologic Compression and the Ice Age

Billion-of-years beliefs are the sustenance of long ages hoped for, the evidence of time imagined.

Russ Miller

Plate Tectonics and Continental Drift

Plate Tectonics is a theory that attempts to explain the large scale movements of our planet's crust which occurred in the unobserved past. This secular interpretation, developed in the early 20th Century, is based on the principle of uniformity that present rates have remained relatively consistent since the beginning of the world, and earth's plates tend to move extremely gradually today through subduction, abduction, and fault shifts.

After observing that the earth's land masses appear to roughly fit together like a jigsaw puzzle, combined with the observation that the land masses scarcely move at all today, Continental Drift was concluded to have taken place uniformly over *millions of years*.

Sea Floor Spreading
By the early 1960s, secular geology generally accepted that the seafloors were gradually and uniformly spreading out along mid-ocean ridges due to volcanic activity, leading to gradual Continental Drift.

Mountain Formation
Old-earth believers observe that today's mountain upheaval tends to occur gradually at about one inch annually. Then, by extrapolating at an assumed uniform rate of uplift in the past, they conclude the mountains formed over *millions of years*.

The biblical view of Plate tectonics, Continental Drift and the formation of mountain ranges is that they required a tremendous worldwide cataclysmic event to occur. The Bible provides us with what that event was: **the global Flood**.

The fountains of the deep erupted at the start of the global deluge and continued pouring forth scalding thermal waters during the first 150 days of the Flood. During this period the land mass was beginning to literally split apart along the ever-widening fissures. This is why the almost 50,000 miles of fault lines found crisscrossing the globe today, which are most likely scars that attest to this event, tend to be found on the world's seafloors. The Mid-Atlantic Ridge is a perfect example.

By the latter stages of the year-long Flood, the heavy fountain waters were on top of the earth's surface, including being on top of the thinner crusts which had been above the fountain waters in the original Creation.

Psalm 104 refers to an event toward the Flood's end when the waters sloshed back and forth from the mountains to the valleys.

8 *They go up by the mountains; they go down by the valleys unto the place which thou hast founded for them.*

I interpret this as the result of the mountains and ocean basins suddenly forming during a massive tectonic event that caused the flood waters to surge back and forth.

A viable scenario is that the thinner crusts eventually gave way to the tremendous weight of water on top of them and collapsed into the nearly emptied fountain chambers. The collapsed areas resulted in today's ocean basins, while some areas were vaulted skyward, forming many of our present mountains. Supporting evidence of this includes that the earth's crust averages about thirty-five miles thick under the continents today, yet only about three miles thick at the bottom of the seas.

It is an observable fact that fossils of marine creatures are found on top of the world's tallest mountains. Of course, the secular, uniformitarian view interprets such marine fossils as proof that the mountains have been gradually uplifted over *millions of years*. However, the fossils actually suggest that the biblical view, that recently deposited flood layers were vaulted skyward toward the end of the Flood to form most of today's mountains, is the correct interpretation of the world we live in.

In Flagstaff, Arizona, at 7,000+ feet elevation, I find fossilized shark teeth, trilobites, sponges, clams and the remnants of other marine creatures strewn about the area. Each fossil is solid supporting evidence of the Scriptural view that most of the earth's geological features are the result of the global Flood.

A biblical view of Continental Drift is that during the same timeframe as the mountains were being lifted upward, the original land mass was violently splitting into sections. These land masses then slid apart from each other and away from the fissures that had been created when the fountains of the deep spewed forth their scalding waters.

This resulted in any Continental Drift observed today as the single continent from the original Creation was now divided into today's multiple land masses. Yes, it really is that simple.

Occam's razor

Some of the land masses halted abruptly, and similar to the hood of a car that smashes into a tree, the surface of the earth crumpled, pushing more mountain ranges upward. Other land masses smashed into one another resulting in additional mountain upheaval. Other plates slid under or over other pieces of land, resulting in the abducted and subducted plates we can observe today.

Geologic Compression

Entire mountain ranges are observed that are made of hundreds of feet of stratified layers of rock. Many of these ranges have been smashed together, resulting in as much as 145-degree folds in the strata layers, yet the rock isn't cracked. These are known as geologic compression events, and they are found all around the globe. If you observe the strata layers along a roadway that has been cut through a hill or mountain range you will often see folded, yet unbroken, rock layers. These are the results of a geologic compression event. So how does a layer of rock become bent, sometimes almost in half, without fracturing the rock?

Relying once again on the unobserved assumption of *uniformity*, old-earth believers claim that, once upon a time, the folded strata layers were subducted over *vast ages of time*. The story continues that, after being forced under the earth's surface, the layers became heated and pliable. This they claim is when the folding occurred. Next, the now-folded rock strata were pushed back to the surface, leaving the compressed yet unbroken layers of rock we can see today.

However, the folded rock strata are sedimentary layers that were laid down by water. Had such a subduction event taken place, the heating of the strata to an extent that it could have become folded without cracking would have metamorphosed the rock. That is, the rock would have been altered from sedimentary rock to metamorphic rock. Yet the layers are still sedimentary. This should be obvious to everyone with a single geology course under their belt, yet this observable fact is totally ignored by secular geology.

The biblical view is that the rock layers aren't broken because they were still soft mud which had been laid down by water shortly before a catastrophic tectonic event smashed them together, folding the stratified mud layers which later hardened into rock. Yes, it really is that simple.

If the simplest answer is generally better than more complex explanations, then geologic compression events support the biblical view that a tremendous tectonic event occurred in conjunction with the worldwide geological event known as the global Flood.

Occam's razor

Secular misinterpretations of mountain formation, Continental Drift, and geologic compression events highlight the fact that uniformity-based thought has undermined scientific research, science education, and the saving faith of billions of people around the world.

The Ice Age(s)

It is a scientific fact that the earth's ice caps once covered much more of the areas surrounding the northern and southern poles than what we see covered in ice today.

The secular interpretation is that our planet has, over billions *of years*, endured several periods of atmospheric cooling. They believe these cooling cycles led to huge amounts of snowfall which covered large regions of the earth's northern and southern hemispheres and resulted in multiple Ice Ages with the most recent Ice Age ending about ten thousand years ago.

The secular view also assumes that glaciers have always moved at the gradual rate we can observe today; uniformity. Based on this mistaken idea, Secularists interpret glacier movement as proof for *millions of years* of time.

The fact is that the snow and ice found on the Polar Regions today represent huge amounts of water. The only viable way to get these tremendous volumes of water to the poles in the form of snowfall would have been by massive cloud transportation, and to form such cloud cover would have required massive evaporation from the world's oceans. However, cooling periods and worldwide Ice Ages would have led to cooler oceans and less evaporation. This would have resulted in less snowfall reaching the poles. When you consider these facts, you realize that the secular view does not make logical sense.

Well, if the ice caps did not form during a cooling cycle of the earth's atmosphere, how did they form?

The biblical view interprets the same ice caps and evidence of glacial activity as being the result of the global Flood.

One viable Scriptural interpretation of the Ice Age includes that during the first 150 days of the Flood, the fountains of the deep were continually spewing forth scalding hot water and molten magmas.

Also, due to the movement of the earth's crust, our planet would have been experiencing unprecedented levels of volcanic activity both during the year-long Flood as well as for hundreds of years following the global catastrophe.

The thermal fountain waters and the volcanic activity combined to warm the flood waters to an average of about 90 degrees Fahrenheit. The warm flood waters led to massive evaporation which created tremendous cloud cover around the globe. These clouds were pouring down rain across the central hemispheres while dumping huge volumes of snowfall on the northern and southern regions of the planet. Thus, the year of the Flood was also the beginning of the Ice Age.

During the first 200 to 300 years following the global Flood, the world's oceans began to slowly cool down. Still, throughout this period of time the warmer oceans continued to produce tremendous amounts of evaporation. The resulting clouds continued to dump rain upon the central hemispheres and large amounts of snow fell across the northern and southern Polar Regions. Glaciers formed rapidly during this timeframe as the planet endured its one and only Ice Age.

From 300 to 700 years after the worldwide Flood ended, ocean temperatures continued to gradually drop until they reached the temperatures we can observe today. During this same period of time, evaporation and cloud cover continued to diminish, and the *Ice Age* came to an end.

Soon the ice caps began to melt, and the ice packs began to retreat northward. A map showing the regions that were covered in ice during the Ice Age support this biblically-based interpretation. Maps reveal that the ice fields once extended south to where northern Kansas is today. However, if you look at a map of today's ice packs, you will see they are 1,500+ miles north of Kansas. The melting of the ice caps has been a 4,000-year process since the Flood waters cooled down to today's temperatures.

An eye-opening fact is that most of the planet enjoyed a tropical climate during the post-Flood Ice Age. Consider the situation. The world's oceans were holding large amounts of heat. The resulting humidity and abundant moisture created a tropical climate that was great for the growth of lush vegetation in the central regions for the first 300 to 700 years following the global deluge.

Have you ever wondered why people settled in the vast desert regions of the Middle East? It is because those areas were receiving tremendous amounts of rainfall throughout the Ice Age that followed the worldwide Flood. Today's Middle Eastern deserts were blanketed by lush grasslands and forests when people began their civilizations there.

The biblical interpretation makes logical sense, while uniformity-based thought gnaws away at people's perception of the truth of God's Word and undermines scientific research and education. The facts are that *billions of years* beliefs are the sustenance of long ages hoped for, the evidence of time imagined.

"I wanted to let you know you have changed my life! I wanted to encourage you and let you know the information you are sharing is making a big difference in people's lives."

Isabella in CA

Section II:
The Top Ten Evil Fruits of Old-Earth Beliefs

Introduction to Chapters 7 -15

Beloved, when I gave all diligence to write unto you of the common salvation, it was needful for me to write unto you, and exhort you that ye should earnestly contend for the faith which was once delivered unto the saints. Jude 1:3

People are saved by God's grace alone through faith alone in Jesus Christ alone. However, once saved, Christians are to be pro-active. We are called to spread the Word and contend for the faith.

Jesus told us to tell good from bad by the fruit, and all Christians should be involved in one of the many battles that are raging around the world and in their own backyards: abortion, drug abuse, the teaching of *billions of years* and Darwinism, pornography, homosexuality, teenage pregnancies, moral relativism—the list seems endless— and each of these issues is a serious matter that needs faithful Christian soldiers in the battle, contending for the faith.

While we do win some of the battles, we are losing the culture war. Why is this so? Allow me to provide some food for thought:

It is because we are fighting the evil fruit but not the evil root.

Think about this. What is the foundation for Secular Humanism? It is Naturalism. Well, what is the foundation of modern-day Naturalism? It is Darwinism. And what is the foundation for Darwinian evolutionism? Old-earth beliefs – *billions of years* of time is the foundation for Darwinism which is the foundation for Naturalism which is the foundation for Humanism. The foundation, the evil root, is *billions of years* of time which places death before mankind undermining the **COS†**: that God's perfect (**C**)reation was corrupted by Adam's (**O**)riginal Sin which (**S**)eparated man from God (while allowing death to enter the world) requiring we be ✝ (the Cross) redeemed with our loving Creator and redeeming Savior, Jesus Christ.

And what two foundational issues have secular public schools pounded into the minds of children since 1963? *Billions of years* and *Darwinism*.

Unfortunately, most Christians, even those who are steadfastly engaged in the battle, do not realize that the root problem is *billions of years*. Because of this we *fight the fruit but not the root* while we lose the war for the eternal souls of billions of people.

Let us heed the wisdom of the Lord Jesus found in Matthew 7:17-20, where the Lord tells us:

Even so every good tree bringeth forth good fruit; but a corrupt tree bringeth forth evil fruit. A good tree cannot bring forth evil fruit, neither can a corrupt tree bring forth good fruit. Every tree that bringeth not forth good fruit is hewn down, and cast into the fire. Wherefore by their fruits ye shall know them.

Because Jesus said we are to tell good from bad by the fruits being produced, my list of the *Top Ten Evil Fruits of Old-Earth Beliefs* will begin with the *Number One* fruit that has grown from the old-earth tree: Darwinism.

I will discuss the *Top Ten Darwinian Predictions or Beliefs* in chapters 7 – 12. Then I will finish my list of the *Top Ten Evil Fruits of Old-Earth Beliefs* in chapters 13 -15, ending with the ultimate fruit of the old-earth tree.

The study of our origins has never been about the evidence. Instead, the study of our origins is about the worldview through which the evidence is interpreted. After all, everyone has the same evidence to test, study and observe.

Scientists, textbook authors, publishers and teachers are people just like you and me, and we each hold religious beliefs. Even an atheist holds to a belief which is that God does not exist. All beliefs (axioms) provide the framework through which people will interpret any evidence they observe. Those holding to a belief in Darwinian-style evolution will see things as having evolved naturally over long ages of time.

1 Thessalonians 5:21 tells us:

Prove all things; hold fast that which is good.

In real science a hypothesis must be realistic in nature and predictable. It must also be refutable, that is, if it fails to meet its own predictions, or if new discoveries undermine the hypothesis, it will be discarded. Keeping this in mind, let's take a look at some information about what I consider to be the _Top Ten Darwinian Predictions or Beliefs_. You will see there are some serious problems with the Darwinian-biased interpretations of the facts. I will also interpret the same evidence through a biblical view.

I think you'll find this section to be eye-opening.

"I'm hosting your DVDs in our adult Sunday school and it's going great! Everyone is really excited! They are engrossed in the messages. Wow, I'm very excited to help get the Truth out!"

Bonnie in CA

Chapter Seven

Earth is 4.6 Billion Years Old;
Life Began on its Own

The revolution (against Christianity) ***began when it became obvious earth was ancient rather than having been created 6,000 years ago. This finding was the snowball that started the whole avalanche.***

   Former Harvard Biology Professor, and atheist, Ernst Mayr.

After I presented my *50 Facts Versus Darwinism In The Textbooks* at Northern Arizona University, a professor offered an accredited course attacking me and biblical Creation. He told me he had been raised in a Christian home, and when he went to college, he became convinced the earth was *billions of years* old, which destroyed his faith in God's Word.

This is because old-earth beliefs put death before Adam. In doing so, old-earth beliefs mean that man's original sin did not bring death into a perfect Creation while separating man from his Creator. Without this separation there is no need for a redeeming Savior, the Lord Jesus. Thus, the authority of God's Word is undermined in the minds of those who accept, and understand the consequences, of old-earth beliefs.

The Earth formed 4.6 billion years ago
Are you still unsure about whether or not the age of the earth matters? I think this section will change your thinking.

Charles Darwin read Lyell's book, *Principles of Geology*. Darwin then took the belief in uniformity and applied it to biology, wrongly thinking that over long ages of time life forms would gradually evolve better and better without God.

As previously noted, *billions of years* is the foundation for Darwinism. These two beliefs, *billions of years* and Darwinism, have combined to practically erase Christian principles from Western Civilization. In fact, the majority of Christian children are leaving the Church by the age of twenty. The misled NAU professor is just one out of the billions of victims.

The Darwinian belief is based on the belief that a molten rock formed as a result of the Big Bang about 4.6 billion years ago. Then oceans formed on the rock as it rained for millions of years and eventually, from this sterile, wet rock, life began by a series of chemical reactions. Of course this does not happen today when we could observe this phenomenon occurring. Oh no, it was long ago and far away.

This conjecture has been taught in science classes for the past fifty years, and it is important to realize that *billions of years* is the foundation for both Darwinism and Big Bang cosmologies.

I covered where the old-earth beliefs come from in Chapters 1 through 6. The truth is that nothing is as far away from reality as a belief in *millions of years* of time unless you believe in *billions of years* of time. Because this is such a key issue, and because a global Flood erodes *death before Adam* beliefs, I will provide more insight into the worldwide Flood in Chapter 20. Please review these chapters for more information on issues regarding the age of the earth.

Life Began on its own

Darwinism predicted biology would find non-living matter spontaneously generating life. This would be reliable, empirical criteria for Darwinism.

To be fair, know that modern-day, Darwinian-biased biologists will throw a fit that I list the start of life as having anything to do with Darwinism. As I often say, Darwinism has undermined real scientific research and scientific education. This is a perfect example.

Biology is supposed to be the *study of life*. However, since Darwinists, who own the educational establishments, believe that life spontaneously arose due to naturally occurring circumstances, and because this has proven to be a scientific impossibility, they now claim that the key presupposition of modern biology, Darwinism and the origin of the species, has nothing to do with the origin of life.

So the primary axiom of the *study of life* has nothing to do with the start of life? Really?

Not to be mean-spirited, but if you believe that a big bang formed a big rock, then it rained on the rock, and here we are today, somewhere along the line you have to believe life began suddenly and on its own. That is spontaneous generation.

The scientific problem for Darwinism, or anyone who believes life began without God, is that we now know non-living matter **cannot** spontaneously generate life. In real biology this is known as the Law of Biogenesis which states that life only comes from life. In other words, Darwinists cannot even get life started. Because of this, Darwinists try to separate the origin of life from their belief in the origin of the species.

To try and get around the Law of Biogenesis, secular textbooks teach that life did not spontaneously generate itself but instead came about through a process of chemical reactions that occurred for *billions of years* until, sometime, somewhere, life came to be. This is known as Abiogenesis. [24]

Though Darwinists scream foul when I point this out, even Abiogenesis requires that a magical moment once occurred when and where the Law of Biogenesis was overcome and life spontaneously began on its own.

But do not just take my word that Darwinian-based biology has no way to get life started. Let me go to the textbook used at Northern Arizona University in the class designed to attack both me and biblical Creation. The author was the atheist president of the *The National Center for Science Education*. Here is her explanation on how life began:

"...the origin of life was not a sudden event but a continuum of events producing structures that...are alive, with a lot of iffy stuff in the middle." [25]

Need I say more? Keep in mind that the unobserved belief that life somehow began due to naturally occurring processes is foundational to Naturalism and Humanism. Since Secularists own the educational, scientific and media establishments, their interpretations of the world, even when in direct conflict with scientific law, are taught in schools around the globe as if they were science.

Untold numbers of experiments have been conducted over the past hundred years to try and get past the Law of Biogenesis.
Building on the findings from previous experiments, with billions of dollars of salaries, computers and lab equipment thrown in, a few well-designed experiments have been able to produce some non-living amino acids, and amino acids are the building blocks for proteins. [26]

However, there are hundreds of types of amino acids and each one comes in right or left-handed versions. The 20 specific amino acids found in life must all be left-handed, with right-handed nucleotide sugars (with a few rare exceptions). Yet the few amino acids that have been made in these well-designed and controlled experiments always have a 50-50 mixture of right and left-handed versions.

Add to this fact that the researchers have to quickly isolate any amino acids that form from the apparatus they designed to form them; otherwise, the conditions they intelligently designed to make the amino acids would quickly destroy the ones that formed. There isn't anything natural about these failed attempts to create life in a lab.

The bottom line is that mankind has not come anywhere close to showing how life could have begun in well-designed lab tests, much less in a natural setting. [27]

Still, secular science books teach that life started on its own in nature and insinuate that life has been created from non-life in laboratory experiments. So beware of science falsely so called. 28

To overcome the scientific Law of Biogenesis, and to get past the *iffy stuff*, Darwinists teach that the first form of life was just a simple cell. As I often point out, real science is a Christian's best friend and research continually discovers there is no such thing as a simple cell.

Observable science has revealed that bacteria cells are run by microscopic motors called *bacterial flagellum* which allow the cell to move around to perform its various functions. These tiny molecular motors are so compactly designed that a billion of them could fit onto the head of a pin.

The flagellum is made of forty different and very specific types of proteins, each protein requiring the appropriate amino acids. These microscopic motors are also *irreducibly complex*. This means that if any of the proteins were not present in the exact order to form the flagellum at the exact moment that life began, life could never have started.

And more daunting for the secular view is that it takes other molecular motors, which are also irreducibly complex, to put the proteins together to form the flagellum in the first place. 29

No wonder the Law of Biogenesis has never been observed to have been violated!

Recognizing the impossibility of life having begun on its own on earth, yet struggling to keep their belief in *billions of years leading to Darwinism* alive, many in the Humanist crowd are choosing to believe that life started somewhere else in the universe and was transported to earth by either aliens or meteorites. No, I am not making this up. This notion, referred to as Panspermia or Transpermia, does not even attempt to explain the origin of life. Instead, the *origin of life* issue is sent far, far away where it is not such an embarrassment to Darwinists and other Naturalists.

As the saying goes, those who choose not to believe in God will believe in anything. Or in this case, those who choose not to believe *In the beginning God created* will believe in the absurd, though they may not admit it.

Today, Darwinists will vehemently deny that the origin of life has anything to do with Darwinism. This is because there is no evidence whatsoever that non-life has ever come to life in a natural setting or in a controlled laboratory environment.

Darwinists predicted that biology would find non-living matter spontaneously generating life. The observable fact is that Darwinism fails its own key criterion so they retreat to their unobservable *billions of years* of time. Somehow enough time makes the impossible seem possible. It really is about time.

Regardless of the actual science, the secular belief that life came about on its own has been taught in the place of real science for over fifty years. This false teaching has undermined scientific research, education and the Christian faith of billions of people.

According to the Word of God in Genesis 2, our Creator ended His work of creating on the seventh day.

2 *And on the seventh day God ended his work which he had made; and he rested on the seventh day from all his work which he had made.*

The biblical view is that God created life during the Creation week, so science will not find life developing from non-life today. The Law of Biogenesis is reliable, empirical criteria in support of Scripture.

Occam's razor.

"I'm 22 years old and was raised as a Christian, but I'm one of the 85% who lost their faith due to what we're taught in college. My mom talked me into attending your seminar and I want you to know that I am back on track with God! Thank you for your ministry."

Ryan in AZ

Chapter Eight

Micro and Macro-evolution

All knowledgeable Christians are evolutionists. We accept biblically correct, and scientifically observable, micro-evolution.

Russ Miller

Did you know that Believers are also evolutionists? Micro-evolutionists, that is.

Darwinists predicted biology would find proof of macro-evolution. Such findings would be reliable, empirical criteria for Darwinism. Because the majority of people who believe in Darwinism do so based on having been misled on what Darwinian-style change really is, let me provide a couple of important definitions. Darwinists hate such clarification as they need to remain elusive on these definitions in order to create confusion and fool people into accepting their belief in Darwinian-style change.

The fact is that the word *evolution* has several meanings, and two of them are vital to understand when it comes to biological evolution. This is because one definition fits exactly with God's Word, while the second meaning is in direct conflict with the Bible. These two types of evolution are *micro* and *macro*.

Micro-evolution is simply variations that occur **within** the same kind of organism. If you were to ask me, "Russ, do you believe in evolution?" I would answer, "I absolutely believe in biblically correct micro-evolution."30

Because of the various definitions of the word *evolution*, it's best to avoid confusion and therefore better to refer to micro-evolution as micro-adaptations. These are simply kinds bringing forth after their own kind. For example, a white dog giving birth to a brown puppy would be a micro-adaptation. Though adaptations within a certain kind can vary widely, kinds will only bring forth after their kind. That is, dogs will only produce dogs, and people will only bring forth people. This is observable evidence in support of God's Word as ten times in the book of

71

Genesis we're told that kinds will bring forth after their kind. For example, in Genesis 1 we are told:

21 *And God created great whales, and every living creature that moveth, which the waters brought forth abundantly, after their kind, and every winged fowl after his kind: and God saw that it was good.*

Millions of examples of micro-adaptations are observed, making micro-change both a biblical truth and a scientific fact. Once again, real science is a Believer's best friend.

Another example of micro-adaptations is when botanists produce roses that grow better in warmer or cooler climates or that produce red or yellow flowers. These micro-adaptations are obtained by employing human intelligence along with Genetic Depletion, the sorting or loss of pre-existing genetic information, to breed out undesired traits. I will discuss this principle more in Chapter Nine.

For instance, by breeding yellow roses with yellow roses, the genetic data to produce other colors is eventually lost (Gene Depletion). From then on the plant will only produce the desired color.[31] This is how purebred cattle, horses, cats and dogs are obtained, by selective breeding in order to lose the genetic information that would express undesired traits.

Because they come about by the accumulating losses of DNA, micro-changes can only bring forth within the same kind of organism. That is, cattle will only bring forth cattle and roses will only bring forth roses. No matter how long they are bred together, the flowers will never produce non-roses such as pine trees, porpoises or parakeets. That would be Darwinian-style evolution, which is scientifically impossible as I will explain in Chapter Nine when I show how to refute Darwinism in 4 seconds.

This brings us to macro-evolution. Macro-evolution is Darwinian-style evolution that requires the random addition of massive amounts of new and beneficial genetic information to an organism's gene pool. And the data must come about by natural processes. I'm talking about the kind of information that would lead to the origin of new kinds of plants and animals, literally the evolution of *goo to you* as promoted in secular schools as if it were science.

For example, a dog evolving into a whale would be a macro-change. In fact, a dog producing a whale's flipper or a blowhole on the top of its head would also be an example of macro-evolution. However, macro-evolution has never been observed except in the creative minds and desperate drawings of the Darwinian faithful. Unfortunately, their unobserved ideas fill secular textbooks. As I like to say, **Darwinists are experts at drawing things that never existed to support their theory which never took place.**

Obviously, had macro-evolution occurred, researchers should be able to produce millions of clear examples from the fossil record or from among the hundreds of millions of plant and animal species that are living today. After all, I could show millions of examples of scripturally correct micro-adaptations (if I wanted to), yet our secular society labels those of us who trust God's Word as being non-scientific.

So shouldn't we expect secular beliefs, which are taught in schools as science, to be held to the same standard and produce some viable evidence in support of what they are teaching?

Absolutely, it's only fair. However, as of this writing, and after millions of observations, Darwinists have no viable evidences to present in support of their *non-scientific* religious belief. Even Charles Darwin never observed a single example of macro-evolution.

While on the Galapagos Islands, Darwin keenly observed thick-billed and thin-billed finches. He saw brown and yellow finches too. He then came to the erroneous conclusion that the finches proved, "*It is a truly wonderful fact...that all animals and all plants throughout all time and space should be related to each other.*"32

You should be thinking, *all Darwin saw were perfect examples of biblically correct micro-adaptations, finches bringing forth finches.*

And you'd be right.

Darwin published his mistaken theory in 1859, and secular researchers have been trying, and failing, ever since to find evidence to support Darwinism. Lacking viable evidence, secular educators like to flow between the definitions of the word *evolution* without explaining the differences. This creates a lot of confusion which Darwinists desire since the straightforward facts don't support what they're teaching.

In the confusion, Darwinists promote their biased interpretations of the facts and dishonestly present examples of micro-adaptations while discussing Darwinian evolution.

The end result is that billions of unsuspecting kids are fooled into thinking that *molecules to man* change took place. And the majority of Christian children are leaving the Church by the age of twenty.

Darwinism predicted biology would find proof of macro-evolution. Darwinism fails to meet its own critical criteria.

Professing themselves to be wise, they became fools, And changed the glory of the uncorruptible God into an image made like to corruptible man, and to birds, and fourfooted beasts, and creeping things. Romans 1:22-23

The biblical view holds that biology will find micro-evolution taking place, and millions of observations show that kinds will only bring forth after their kind. God's Word meets its critical criteria.

"My friend, a science major attended your message at my church. Though he was mad at you afterward, within two weeks he admitted you were just telling the truth and his faith in God has grown dramatically." Eli in TN

"We were certainly blessed to have you here...many people have told me their eyes were opened to biblical truth. Many who held to varying forms of theistic evolution have expressed joy in finding the truth." Pastor Will Stoll

Chapter Nine

New and Beneficial Genetic Information; Natural Selection

Empirical science knows of no way for complex information to form without an extreme source of intelligence having designed it. When it comes to genetic information, other than iffy stuff and alien conspiracies, the silence coming from the Secular camp is deafening.　　　　Russ Miller

Do you have a hero? Darwinists have two: mutations and time.

Since non-observed macro-evolution requires random additions of massive amounts of new and beneficial genetic information to an organism's gene pool, let's discuss how Darwinists propose this occurs.

Neo-Darwinism is the belief that the required genetic information is acquired through mutations. Such findings would be reliable, empirical criteria for Darwinism.

Unless you are currently enrolled in a biology course or have a keen interest in genetics, this chapter may go into more detail than you want to know. However, because this is a frontline issue in Darwinian biased biology, I want to provide some insight into the world of genetics.

With the scant evidence Darwinists have been promoting for the past fifty years being refuted on a regular basis, Darwinists have gone inside the cell. They are literally saying, "Hey, if you had your own electron microscope you would see the proof for Darwinism, but since you don't, just take our word for it." Unfortunately, history and real science reveal we cannot take their word for much of anything, so let's review the facts.

The DNA of any kind of living organism is made of four chemicals that are represented by the letters A, T, C and G. How these chemicals are arranged make up specific instructions, called genes, which are extremely complex genetic instructions that allow the organism to mend, grow and reproduce more of its kind. Chromosomes hold the DNA, and an organism's entire DNA comprises its genome.

But DNA cannot form without proteins, and proteins cannot form without DNA. I discussed the impossibility of proteins forming on their own and the Law of Biogenesis in Chapter 7, so for the sake of moving ahead, I will pretend that multiple bacteria cells managed to come to life on their own. However, that just brings us to another major problem for Darwinism: **information.**

The fact is that *bacteria to Beethoven* evolution requires there to be naturally occurring processes that add huge amounts of new and beneficial genetic information to an existing gene pool. I am talking about genetic data that would cause a bacteria cell to change into all the millions of life forms that have ever lived on our planet.

Where did the original genetic information come from?

To avoid getting into more *iffy stuff* or *alien conspiracies* I will let Darwinists off the hook and not demand to know where the original genetic information came from. This is extremely generous of me, as real science knows of no way whatsoever for complex information to come about on its own in a natural environment. All observations show that complex information must be derived from a source of extreme intelligence.

Darwinian evolution itself failed due to its inability to provide a naturally occurring mechanism that could add massive amounts of new and beneficial genetic information to existing gene pools. Since nothing was known about genetic information in Darwin's day, that is not a big surprise. However, now that we have a basic understanding of genetics and are beginning to have a clue as to the extreme complexity of genetic data and its ability to function, it is surprising any geneticist, biologist or micro-biologist still thinks life developed by random accident.

Lacking a way to generate the needed genetic data, Darwinists came up with what is called Neo-Darwinism. Taught as science in schools today, this is the belief that genetic mutations create the new and beneficial genetic data needed to power *paramecium to pine tree* evolution. The story continues that the improved mutant takes over its population as Natural Selection eliminates its weaker, non-mutated colleagues. Then, over *billions of years*, mutations changed that first single-celled organism into every living plant or animal which has ever existed on the earth.

This belief holds that all parts of all living beings came about piece by piece. Whether we are talking about the beak of a bluebird, or the brain, central nervous system, or eye of a biology professor, Neo-Darwinists believe everything came about due to random mutations adding massive amounts of new and beneficial genetic information to the ancestor's gene pools.

Since this is taught as science in schools around the world, I think it is fair to expect Darwinists to present thousands of undeniable examples of nature adding new and beneficial genetic information to pre-existing gene pools. Correct? However, there has never been a single scientific experiment or observation that has shown a viable example of a natural process adding appreciable amounts of new and beneficial genetic information to a creature's DNA.

Genetic Depletion

In fact, all observations show that mutations are caused by the sorting or loss of pre-existing genetic information. Furthermore, all variations or adaptations are also caused by the sorting or loss of the DNA inherited from the parents. This is a principle known as Genetic Depletion.

I will discuss how Gene Depletion and another observable principle combine to make Darwinism a scientific impossibility later in this chapter.

For now, note that I said there has never been a *viable* example of a natural process adding appreciable amounts of new and beneficial genetic information to a creature's DNA. I did not say that Darwinists do not present examples. There is a big difference.

Darwinists lack viable examples because mutations in the DNA strand occur due to the sorting or loss of the parent's pre-existing genetic information (Gene Depletion), not from the gain of new and beneficial genetic data.

Beneficial mutations

Darwinists will often point to a mutation that may have resulted in some type of benefit to the mutant as proof of nature having added new and beneficial genetic information to the mutant's DNA. This is simply dishonest. Even in an extremely rare case where a mutation benefited the mutant, the change was still caused by the sorting or loss of genetic information, not by the gain of new and beneficial data. 33

For example, if a wild boar living on a brush-choked island were to lose the genetic data to form its parents' 16 inch long legs due to a mutation in its DNA, and instead had legs just 15 inches long, that mutation would be a benefit if the shorter legs allowed it to duck under the brush faster to escape the leopard hunting it.

Though this mutation would have resulted in a benefit for the boar, like virtually all observed mutations, it would have been caused by the loss of genetic information, not from the gain of new and beneficial data.

Nylon-eating bacteria are often given as an example of Neo-Darwinism in action. Initially, in the 1970's when b a c t e r i a were discovered that could digest nylon, this was just a misinterpretation of the evidence. Based on their starting axiom that things evolve better and better due to mutations, Darwinists immediately assumed a mutation had added new and beneficial genetic information to the bacterium's DNA.

However, by the mid-1990s research had proven that the bacterium's ability to digest nylon was caused by a mutation that caused a loss of function in a protein-degrading enzyme. This loss of genetic data resulted in them feeding on nylon. [34]

So nylon-eating bacteria began as bacteria and ended as bacteria with less useful genetic information than their parent form had, and this loss of data was passed on to other bacteria by plasmid transfers.

Plasmid transfers

Another Darwinian claim has to do with the fact that certain types of bacterium can transfer small amounts of genetic data from one bacterium to another. These are referred to as plasmid transfers, and Darwinists claim that, given *billions of years*, these exchanges lead to Darwinian change.

Research does show plasmid transfers can increase the amount of DNA in an existing organism. However, these genetic exchanges only transfer pre-existing genetic data; they don't create new information. The data must already exist in one bacterium so it is available to be transferred to another bacterium.[35] Also, the bacteria begin with genetic information found in bacteria and end up with the same, only in another bacterium. This will not lead to worms or wooly mammoths no matter how long it was to continue. Therefore, plasmid transfers have nothing to do with the creation of new and beneficial genetic information as required to cause bacteria to macro-evolve into non-bacteria.

All of the misleading claims lead me to ask, **"Why don't they bring out the real examples of nature adding the required new and beneficial data to a gene pool?"** The only viable answer is that there are no such examples to show.

It is important to understand that adding new genetic information is not what Darwinism requires. To propel a bacteria cell to change into a giraffe would require **massive amounts of both new and beneficial genetic data**, not just new data. Any new genetic information would need to add discernible benefits to the mutant so Natural Selection could favor it over its kin.

Darwinists mislead students by discussing instances of new genetic data being added without pointing out it is harmful or has no effect on the mutant. So keep in mind that any data must be new and it must provide a benefit to the mutant in order to have any chance of leading to Darwinian-style change.

Gene Duplication

For example, Darwinists claim that Genetic Duplication produces new and beneficial genetic data. So what does scientific research reveal?

Well, while rare Genetic Duplication errors do occur in nature, they do not create new and beneficial genetic data; they simply copy *pre-existing data*. This is why they're called duplication or copying errors.

As an example, take fruit flies which, in labs, are subjected to radiation in order to cause genetic mistakes to occur. If you've ever seen a picture of a fruit fly with four wings, then you've likely seen the results of Genetic Duplication.

The extra wings are useless as they won't have all of the pieces that function and allow it to fly. Because of the genetic copying error, the fly can't fly and in a natural setting, the four-winged fruit fly would be the one most likely removed by Natural Selection.

Also, consider the printing of this book. If a printing press malfunctioned and made two copies of page 34, would that add any new information to the book? Of course not — copying errors just make copies of what was already there; they don't add new or beneficial information.36 *Gene Duplication does not lead to Darwinian-style evolution.*

Once you grasp the fact that Darwinism requires **massive amounts of both new and beneficial genetic data** in order for a bacteria cell to change into a rose bush, not just new genetic information alone, you will not be fooled when Darwinists propose a small handful of examples where genetic mutations have added new data to an existing gene pool. This is because, in these extremely rare cases, the mutation did not result in any benefit to the mutant. Therefore, Natural Selection did not have anything to select in order to cause the mutant to take over the gene pool.

In the remainder of this chapter, I will cover many of the claims Darwinists make to fool biology students into thinking the required genetic information is routinely added to existing DNA. Because these are the claims that are misleading so many up-and-coming scientists, including Christian students who want to go into a field of science, I want to provide some information for those seeking the truth. I think this will help you come to realize the level of deceit being employed to fool students into believing we evolved without God.

Following are some easy to understand examples of the two most common examples that Darwinists provide of genetic mutations: *frame shift* and *point mutations.* In these over-simplified examples, the genetic data will be represented by these simple three-letter words: The day was hot. The hot day had one sun. The sun was hot the one day.

Frame shift mutations

A frame shift mutation is usually harmful to the mutated creature, and the most typical kinds of frame shift mutations are caused by the insertion of data where it wasn't designed to be or by the deletion of data. Though both result in new genetic information, the new data is not readable to the creature's DNA system.

In our example, if a b were **inserted** at the beginning of the second sentence, it would read: The day was hot. Bth eho tda yha don esu nth esu nwa sho tth eon eda y.

Though several *new* words, such as eho, sho, and eda, were indeed produced by the mutation, thirteen words and the meaning of two entire sentences were lost. Therefore, even though the DNA strand became longer and produced what could technically be called new words, the overall effect of this insertion mutation was the loss of functional genetic data.

In our example, if the first letter of the first sentence were **deleted**, the other letters would shift to the left and we'd end up with: Hed ayw ash ott heh otd ayh ado nes unt hes unw ash ott heo ned ay. Again, technically speaking, several *new words* were produced but seventeen useful words and the meaning of the information was lost. The result of this mutation was the loss of useful genetic data.

Frame shift mutations are caused by the sorting or loss of the parent's pre-existing genetic information, not from the gain of both new and beneficial data.

Point mutations

A point mutation causes just one letter to be changed in the genetic sequence.

Point mutations result in a loss of useful information, and they can be extremely devastating to the mutant.

In our example, if a point mutation changed the word day to duy, we'd end up with: The duy was hot. The hot duy had one sun. The sun was hot the one duy.

This point mutation added a useless word and lost both a meaningful word and the meaning of the information.

Point mutations are caused by the sorting or loss of the parent's pre-existing genetic information, not from the gain of both new and beneficial data.

Again I ask, why don't Darwinists bring out the real examples of natural processes adding the required new and beneficial data to a gene pool? The only viable answer is that they don't have any to show.

Homeo Box mutations

Darwinists also claim that mutations in Homeo Box genes, known as Hox genes for short, lead to the evolution of new kinds of plants or animals. However, a mutation in the Hox gene, if not immediately fatal, results in a creature that is the weakest of its kind.

Similar to the way a traffic cop directs the flow of cars, Hox genes direct the flow of genetic data.

For example, a cow's DNA contains the genetic information to form its left front leg. This data requires the Homeo Box gene to direct it to the proper place to form the leg. If you have ever seen a picture of a cow with one of its legs protruding from the middle of the poor critter's back, then you've likely observed the result of a Hox gene mutation.

Such a misplaced leg won't have the necessary muscles or nerves to be useful. It will, however, use up resources to maintain it, making the cow the weakest in the herd, and in a natural setting, the more likely to be removed by Natural Selection.

As you can see, real science debunks the wishful thinking of desperate Darwinists who claim that mutations create new and beneficial genetic information, leading to Neo-Darwinian change. Neo-Darwinism predicted biology would find that mutations add massive amounts of new and beneficial genetic information to the gene pools of living organisms. Darwinism once again fails its own critical criteria.

This has left Darwinists desperately groping to find a way that nature might create new and beneficial genetic information. Their desperation has opened the doors to any and all suggestions whose acceptance has undermined real science.

The biblical view is that God created the genetic information found within His created kinds of plants and animals during the Creation week, so science will not find appreciable amounts of new and beneficial genetic data being made today. This is what real science finds and is reliable, empirical criteria in support of God's Word.

Natural Selection

Neo-Darwinism predicted biology would find that Natural Selection, acting on new and beneficial genetic information added to a plant or animal's gene pool by mutations, caused a bacteria cell to eventually improve and evolve into all of the millions of life forms ever to have lived on the earth.

However, as previously pointed out in this chapter, observable evidence proves mutants are the genetically weaker of their kind. Again, this is due to Gene Depletion; mutations and variations are caused by the sorting or loss of the parent's genetic information. Gene Depletion is why mutations are the ones most likely removed by Natural Selection which can only select from traits that are actually exhibited in any given population. This is exactly the opposite of what Neo-Darwinists claim. [37]

For an example, let's return to the brush-choked island. Suppose a wild boar living on the island experienced a genetic mutation that resulted in it losing the genetic data to form its parent's four 16-inch-long legs. Instead, the mutant boar developed just three 16-inch-long-legs and one leg that was just 14 inches long. The result would be that the mutant is the slowest pig on the peninsula, and when the leopard comes along, the mutant is likely the first of its kind to be removed by Natural Selection.

By putting these principles together I came up with why Darwinism has never been observed, as well as how to scientifically debunk Darwinism in 4 seconds flat:

Gene Depletion + Natural Selection make Darwinism a scientific impossibility. [38]

The lack of viable evidence in support of Darwinism is not due to it being lost in the *iffy stuff*. It's because Gene Depletion and Natural Selection combine to make Darwinism scientifically impossible.

Gene Depletion fits well with the Second Law of Thermodynamics, which I discussed in Chapter One. This scientific law holds that all things are losing energy, wearing down. This is the most accepted law in all of the fields of science, except for evolutionary biology. Darwinists have to go against scientific principle because they do not wish to admit their belief is not scientifically viable.

Of course Darwinists need an excuse to explain why this scientific law does not apply to Darwinism, so they invoke the *open system* argument. Darwinists claim that the Law of Entropy does not apply to our solar system because it is an open system which receives large amounts of new energy from the sun.

A fair question is: *If the Law of Entropy doesn't apply to our solar system, how did we discover it?*

Regarding the claim that the Second Law doesn't apply to an *open system* Dr. John Ross of Harvard said, "...the second law applies equally to open systems... It is important to make sure that this error does not perpetuate itself." [39]

Ask yourself this: If you leave a bicycle in the yard for five years, will the sunshine make it better or will the raw energy cause the paint to fade and the plastic parts to crack? In reality, raw energy tends to speed up entropy.

With regard to biology, Darwinists are missing the point. The key issue isn't the energy available to a system, but what *genetic information* is available to it. It's a fact that raw energy, like sunlight, is incapable of producing the complex genetic data found in DNA. It's this information that forms the biological systems that can take raw sunlight and direct it to a useful function, such as in the process of photosynthesis.

Neo-Darwinism predicted biology would find that Natural Selection, acting on new and beneficial genetic information added to existing gene pools by mutations, caused a bacteria cell to eventually improve and evolve into all of the millions of life forms ever to have lived on the earth. But real science, based on actual observations, reveals that mutations, if not immediately fatal, are either neutral or genetically weaker. The neutral mutations have no impact on a kind's gene pool while weaker ones are eliminated by Natural Selection. Once again Darwinism fails its own key criteria.

The biblical view, based more on my interpretation in this case, is that God created the genetic information found within His created kinds of plants and animals during the Creation week and implemented a system that would act to preserve it.

I consider Natural Selection to be God's Quality Assurance program. If genetic losses went unchecked, they would soon lead to the extinction of the plant and animal kinds God made during His week-long Creation. But because of Natural Selection, once a gene pool becomes overly corrupted, it is removed from the population of its particular kind by God's Quality Assurance program.

"I saw Russ share his '50 Facts versus Darwinism' when I was thirteen years old. Six years later, I was studying biochemistry in college. I would have had my faith undermined several times but each time I remembered back to the things Russ revealed in his teaching. That evening, many years before, allowed me to hang on to my faith."

Irene in AZ

Chapter Ten

Similarities and the Fossil Record

I drive a Chevy truck while my friend has a Chevy van, and their dashboards are identical. This isn't because they both evolved from a skateboard!

Russ Miller

Common Ancestry

Darwinism holds that all plant and animal life has descended from a common single-celled ancestor. Darwinists predicted scientists would be able to use the similarities that exist between various kinds of living organisms to track them back to their common ancestor. This would be reliable, empirical criteria of Darwinian evolutionism.

Since Secularists own the educational and science establishments, their biased interpretations of the world are taught as if they were scientific facts. Here is an example from a high school biology book: *All the many forms of life on Earth today are descended from a common ancestor, found in a primitive population of unicellular organisms.*[40]

As you can see, this is presented as a proven fact which unsuspecting high school students assume is backed up by evidence. But what evidence supports this teaching? Well, the answer is given a few sentences later: *No traces of those events remain...*[41]

Actually, a biased interpretation of evidence requires there to be some evidence on which one's bias can be projected. In this example there is no evidence to interpret, so Darwiniacs simply make up what they believe took place and teach their belief as if it were scientific fact.

Note that, from the Big Bang to the primordial oceans to the origin of life to the *common ancestor, found in a primitive population of unicellular organisms...no traces of those events remain.* So much for science being knowledge derived from the study of evidence.

The fact is that *billions of years* and *Darwinism* are two religious beliefs that have combined to undermine scientific research, education, and the Christian faith of billions of people. And again, Darwinism fails its own key criteria.

The biblical view is that we did not evolve from a single-celled anything, so we should not find any evidence of such macro-evolution taking place. Once again the biblical view fits perfectly with what real science observes.

Since there is no evidence that any plant or animal life evolved from the imaginary single-celled ancestor, I will move further along into the tale of Darwinism.

Similarities

The science of Homology looks at similar characteristics between plants and animals. Once again, keep in mind that it is not a matter of the evidence (as long as evidence does exist, that is). Rather, the issue is the worldview through which the evidence is interpreted. Because the secular worldview holds that all plant and animal life has descended from a common ancestor, Darwinists interpret similarities as proof for their religious belief.

Similar bone structure

For example, schoolbooks are adorned with the drawings of the bone structure in a whale's flipper, a cat's leg, a human's forearm and the foreleg of a dog. Since each has two bones in the forelimb, students are taught that this proves they all evolved from a common ancestor. But is it really proof for Darwinian change? [42]

No! Though this has misled millions of unsuspecting kids, it's just the interpretation of the evidence via the secular worldview.

The biblical view of the exact same evidence is that similarities support that we have the same Intelligent Biblical Designer.

Think about it: I drive a Chevy truck while my friend has a Chevy van, and their dashboards are identical. This isn't because they both evolved from a skateboard! The similarities are due to having had the same Designer!

Once again we see that it isn't a matter of who has the evidence because we all have the same facts to consider; the issue is through which worldview the observable facts get interpreted.

Similar biochemistry

Darwinists teach through the public school system that human biochemistry is 98% similar to that of a chimpanzee, proving that we're close evolutionary relatives. The supposed similarities are based on small sections of the DNA strands coupled with ignoring areas of wide discrepancies. Conducting their studies this way provides Darwinists with the results they want while undermining real science.

However, as real, observable science gets into the entire genome, the wider the differences become. During 2010, the chimpanzee genome was finally decoded and many discoveries did not support the claim that we are 98% similar. For instance, chimp DNA is actually 12% longer than human DNA. Also, both humans and chimps have hundreds of ORFan (Open Reading Frame) genes, many of which are crucial to survival. Yet these ORFan genes have a 0% genetic match between man and ape.

Nature journal reported up to a 30% difference exists between the male Y chromosomes of humans and apes. [43] Other research reported that human biochemistry is 75% the same as a worm and 50% the same as a banana! I have not seen these figures reported in any textbooks as I suspect Darwinists did not find them to be very *appealing*. [44]

I see similarities in paintings as proof of a common painter and the **biblical view** interprets similarities in biochemistry as supporting evidence that we have the same Intelligent Biblical Designer.

For textbooks to continue to promote the 98% figure is simply dishonest and begs the question: Why don't Darwinists get rid of the misleading claims and show the real evidence that supports their belief? The only answer is that they do not have any such evidence because, as I explained in Chapter 9:

Gene Depletion + Natural Selection make Darwinism a scientific impossibility.

Darwinian trees of life

Darwinists are experts at drawing things that never existed to promote their theory that never took place and the Darwinian *trees of life* are another good example of this fact. These eye-catching drawings adorn biology textbooks. Some are based on similarities (real or imagined is another issue) in bone structure while others are based on similarities in biochemistry. 45

It is important to note that Darwinists claim similarities in either body structure or in biochemistry to be some of the best proofs of Darwinian descent.

Whether based on similarities in the bone structure or in the biochemistry, the *tree of life* has a supposed common ancestor at the base of the tree. Colorful lines then run from the ancestor to various creatures, supposedly representing their evolutionary paths which Darwinists claim to have figured out based on the similarities.

However, these trees have set Darwinism up for yet another huge fall. This is because if you compare a *tree of life* based on body structure to a *tree of life* based on biochemical similarities, you will discover that the two *trees of life* do not show the same paths of descent among the creatures they present. In fact, the paths shown by the two comparisons of similarities are vastly different from one another!

That's right. Comparisons of the two types of *trees of life* reveal different paths of supposed descent. In other words, similarities in either body structure or in biochemistry do not provide proof of Darwinian descent.

The situation begs the question: Does taking a box of crayons and drawing colorful lines connecting creatures together really prove that they evolved from one another? Of course not!

To be an accurate representation of Darwinism in action, each of the lines would need to be backed up by innumerable transitional fossils. These transitional fossils would need to clearly reveal the evolutionary path from the claimed common ancestor to whatever it supposedly evolved into, yet the few claimed transitional fossils do no such thing.

Darwinists predicted scientists would be able to use biochemical and structural similarities to track organisms back to their common ancestor. Darwinism fails this key criterion.

Convergent evolution: a Darwinian dilemma

To avoid the fact that similarities often fail to be explicable within the Darwinian paradigm, Darwinists have been claiming *convergent evolution* occurred. This means that differing kinds of organisms just happened to evolve similar body structures or biochemistry completely independently of the other. That is, their similarities DO NOT have anything to do with evolution from a common ancestor.

This is a **huge dilemma** for Darwinism because Darwiniacs claim that similarities are one of their strongest proofs of common descent!

The Fossil Record

Believing that earth's strata layers formed slowly and uniformly over *billions of years*, while all life forms slowly evolved from a single-celled creature, Darwinists predicted the fossils found in the rock layers would provide an orderly record of Darwinian evolution.

So what does the fossil record reveal? Well, the fossil record has proven to be yet another embarrassment to Darwinism. For example, Living Fossils are creatures that are alive today yet are exactly like their fossilized ancestors found in strata layers supposedly hundreds of millions of years old. According to the observable evidences, life forms did not evolve slowly over *billions of years*. Claims to the contrary are simply based upon wishful thinking, and supported by bluff and bluster.

The fossil record is not a friend to the tale of Darwinism and the global Flood explains how the strata layers containing the fossil record formed quickly and recently.

The Cambrian Explosion

All of the basic body types (phyla) of plants and animals appear suddenly in the Cambrian layer. This is the lowest layer that contains appreciable numbers of fossils, and there are not any transitional links found in the Cambrian layer. There are no transitionals between the single-celled creatures and any of the phyla nor are there any fossils linking the body types to a common ancestor. This is known as the Cambrian Explosion as each of the basic body designs suddenly appears in the Cambrian layer.

Transitional fossils

Darwinism predicted that the fossil record would be filled with millions of transitional kinds (missing links) revealing our evolutionary past. These would be reliable, empirical criteria of Darwinism.

For example, had a fish evolved into an amphibian we should find thousands of clearly identifiable transitional fossils that show the change as a fin gradually evolved into the shoulder, elbow, ankle, toes and claws of an amphibian's leg. And not just one leg, but four, and not just the skeletal changes but also the needed muscular, nerve and vascular requirements.

Charles Darwin knew that the fossil record did not support his theory during his lifetime. He wrote: *Geology assuredly does not reveal any such finely graduated organic chain...*46

Darwin knew that the fossil record would eventually be developed to the point of either proving or refuting his idea. He wrote: *If my theory be true, numberless intermediate varieties... must assuredly have existed.* 47 Darwin was correct about the fossil record eventually proving or refuting his idea, as the fossil record does indeed refute Darwinism.

You may be thinking, *Come on Russ, I was shown the horse and whale evolution series when I was in school.* Well, you may have been shown the drawings of some misleading Darwinian-biased interpretations of fossils and fragments of fossils. For example, let's take a look at the horse and whale evolution series since schoolbooks and museums still promote them.

The horse fossil series depicts a supposed small ancient horse followed by a series of ever-larger horses evolving into the modern horse. Though the series is convincing, folks are not told the modern horse has been found in strata layers below the supposed ancient horse. Also, all of the museum displays that I'm aware of are made from the bones of modern horses ranging in age from one month to twenty years old.48 Darwinists have lined up the skeletons of modern horses by their size and fooled people around the world into believing in *billions of years leading to Darwinism.*

As we are told in 1 Timothy 6:20-21: ***Timothy, keep that which is committed to thy trust, avoiding profane and vain babblings, and oppositions of science falsely so called.***

The whale series depicts an extinct land mammal next to Ambulocetus which Darwinists claim is the missing link between the land dweller and the whales, followed by a whale. Though this has fooled millions of people into believing in *billions of years leading to Darwinism*, Ambulocetus is pieced together from fossils that came from different strata layers found in different locations. The interpretation of the evidence depends on the reliability of the Darwinists interpreting the fragments [49] and I think I have shown how unreliable their biased opinions can be. Sadly, the misleading Darwinian-biased interpretations of fossil evidence are unrelenting, and the whale series has led millions of people to doubt the authority of Scripture.

On April Fool's Day of 2006, the media proclaimed Tiktaalik roseae as the missing link between fish and amphibians.[50] *Nature* reported the fossils *represent an intermediate between fish with fins and tetrapods with limbs*. However, another article in the same journal stated, Tiktaalik *are straightforward fishes.*[51] Yet Tiktaalik adorns science books today as a transitional fossil.

A fair question is, why don't Secularists remove the frauds and misleading information from the schoolbooks and put in the real proof of *billions of years leading to Darwinism*? The only viable answer is that they don't have any.

The missing transitional links have always been an embarrassment to the religious philosophy of Darwinism. In the 1930s Richard Goldschmidt tried to excuse the missing evidence with the Hopeful Monster Theory. He claimed that transitional links were missing because Darwinian change occurred too quickly to allow any to be caught in the fossil record. For example, he said that *birds may have hatched from reptile eggs*, so no observable evidence existed.

In his book, *Evolution*, the late Dr. Colin Patterson of the British Museum of Natural History did not provide a single transitional link. When asked why, he answered, "I will lay it on the line; there is not one such fossil for which one could make a watertight argument." [52]

By 1980 there was still no viable fossil evidence of Darwinism in action, so renowned Darwinists Niles Eldridge of the Chicago Museum of Natural History and Marxist professor Stephen Gould of Harvard adapted the Hopeful Monster Theory and re-titled it Punctuated Equilibrium. 53

Though Punctuated Equilibrium does sound daunting, all it means is there is no evidence of Darwinism in the fossil record. The change from the Hopeful Monster Theory is that Darwinism didn't occur overnight, but instead it happened in short bursts of time that left no evidence in the fossil record! Dr. Gould wrote: *The absence of fossil evidence for intermediary stages...has been a persistent and nagging problem for gradualistic accounts of evolution.* 54

Darwinism predicted that the fossil record would be filled with millions of *missing links* revealing our evolutionary past. Once again Darwinism fails to meet its own criteria. Whether Darwinists invoke hopeful monsters, punctuated equilibrium or the *iffy stuff*, the fact is that the transitional links are missing.

The secular view is there is no evidence of Darwinism because macro-evolution occurred too quickly to leave any observable evidence behind.

The biblical view is there is no evidence of Darwinism because Gene Depletion + Natural Selection make Darwinian-style evolution a scientific impossibility.

Occam's Razor

Regardless of the observable scientific fact that the transitional links are non-observable, Darwinists own the educational and scientific establishments and continue to draw things that never existed to promote their religious beliefs that never took place.

Living Transitional Kinds

If life had evolved over *billions of years*, Darwinism should be readily observable in the form of transitional kinds of plants and animals from among the hundreds of millions of living species found on earth today.

For example, we should find the fish with a leg in the place of a fin, or a reptile with a feathered wing, or perhaps a monkey that can talk. If you think that I'm joking, you're partly right and partly wrong...perhaps you're evolving! Living transitional kinds would be observable evidence of Darwinism in action, yet none exist. Darwinists claim this is because macro change occurs slowly over *billions of years* of time, so it cannot be observed in the present.

This begs a question:

Does Darwinian evolution occur too quickly to leave evidence in the fossil record, or does it happen too slowly to be observed in the present?

The scientific answer is there is no observable evidence of Darwinism in action because *Gene Depletion + Natural Selection* make Darwinism a scientific impossibility.

The biblical answer is that God made all things during His week-long Creation and rested on the seventh day.

"I hold an advanced degree in biology. I attended the conference and planned to email you my feedback. I didn't think it was going to be very nice. The scientist in me has struggled with Creation. The arguments for it seemed oversimplified and uneducated. I wanted to know how you would explain carbon dating; antibiotic-resistant bacteria; why human fetuses have gill pouches; why a bat wing has bones similar to the human hand. I arrived ready to fight for evolution.

Then Russ began his presentation which got into the details of why Darwinism cannot be true. I was amazed that he addressed every question I had in a very educated, reasonable and scientific manner which he supported with further proof from the Bible. When he finished, I realized I had been completely misled by faulty secular teachings." Ann in MI

Chapter Eleven

Dinosaurs to Birds; Primates to Humans

There is not much pride when you're trapped inside a slowly sinking ship, so Darwinian evangelists keep making unfounded claims to keep their sinking beliefs afloat.

Russ Miller

Dinosaurs Evolved into Birds

Have you ever wanted something so desperately that you made a complete fool out of yourself before admitting it was not meant to be?

Because birds exist today while dinosaurs have become extinct, Darwinists believe that the *terrible lizards* evolved into birds.
Evidence that this has taken place would be reliable, empirical criteria of Darwinism, and Darwinists point at the similarities between some birds and dinosaurs as their proof. For instance, most dinosaurs did lay eggs and some had bird-like feet (though a bit larger). Also, some dinosaur hips had a common design with that found in birds.

This is really another worn out argument that similarities prove things evolved from a common ancestor. In actuality, similarities among different kinds are better proof they have the same Intelligent Biblical Designer.

Dinosaurs are classified into two categories based on their hips: Ornithischians and Saurischians. Saurischians included four-footed giants such as the sauropods and bipedal dinosaurs like T-Rex. Ornithischians, such as Parasaurolophus, had bird-like hips. However, Darwinists don't think that birds evolved from the Ornithischians. Instead, they claim that some Saurischians evolved into birds. [55]

Two facts that conflict with the Darwinian belief are that dinosaurs and bird fossils have been found in the same strata layers. This proves they co-existed. Second, not a single viable transitional fossil of a reptile changing into a bird has ever been discovered.

Since Darwinists have presented several supposed examples of feathered dinosaurs and others that were supposedly developing feathers, let's take a closer look at their interpretations of the evidences.

First, whether a feathered dinosaur has ever been found is MOST debatable. Several bird experts say that the supposed feathered dinosaurs were not dinosaurs in any way, shape or form, but were just flightless birds.

Second, whether a dinosaur with structures that were evolving into feathers has ever been found is truly in the mind of the beholder. Hair-like structures must be interpreted as being *proto-feathers* and Darwinian bird expert Alan Feduccia thinks that *proto-feathers* are really nothing more than degraded fragments of skin.[56]

Unfortunately, the misleading and fraudulent claims hit the front pages around the globe, and after misleading billions of people, quietly disappear.

After one much-promoted *reptile to bird* candidate was exposed as a fraud put together by a Chinese farmer, *USA TODAY* reported: *...this true missing link...sprouted its...tail not 120 million years ago but only shortly before being smuggled out of China.*[57]

This brings me to the infamous Archaeopteryx, claimed to be a transitional link between reptiles and birds even though scientists have found the bones of modern birds "*...farther down the geologic column than Archaeopteryx...*"[58]

Since Darwinists believe that strata layers formed over long ages of time, finding the remains of modern birds in layers below those that contain Archaeopteryx should have refuted it being a transitional link. Yet Archaeopteryx, which had fully developed feathers, is still promoted as a transitional link between reptiles and birds 59 by some Darwinists or as a feathered dinosaur by others.

Another blow to Darwinism is that many of their proto-feathered dinosaurs, those that are supposedly evolving feathers, are found in strata above the layers holding Archaeopteryx and the other feathered bird remains. This means that, according to old earth beliefs, fully formed feathers existed before the proto-feathers!

Though many Darwinists believe dinosaurs evolved into birds, their misinterpreted evidence has not held up to scientific scrutiny. This fact has not stopped this Darwinian tale from being taught in the place of actual science while misleading billions of people into believing that proof for Darwinian-style evolution has been found. So beware of science falsely so called.

The biblical view is that God created birds on the fifth day of the week-long Creation and dinosaurs on the sixth day; therefore, no viable evidence will be found of dinosaurs having evolved into birds. As of this writing, the observable science supports the Word of God (and I expect this trend will continue).

Primates Evolved Into Humans

Darwinists believe that apes and humans (*Homo sapiens*) evolved from an ancient common ancestor. Proof of this would be reliable, empirical criteria of Darwinism.

Ask a Darwinist why we still have apes if they evolved into humans, and you'll be told it's because we didn't evolve directly from apes. Instead, we had a common primate ancestor from which apes branched off one way while mankind forked off in another direction.

That sounds somewhat reasonable if you believe you evolved in the first place. However, this begs the logical question:

If we didn't evolve from apes, why do Darwinists spend so much time trying to find bones that will convince people that we did evolve from apes? After all, we have all been shown the Hominids which are supposed to be the closest evolutionary link between ape and man. Since they have all been quietly shown to be an ape, a human, or a fraud, let's review some of them here.

Neanderthal Man was first found in Germany's Neander Valley in 1856. Though many Darwinists still claim Neanderthal was a link between ape and man, the facts show otherwise.

For instance, Neanderthals held religious ceremonies and interbred with modern man. Their brain was larger than ours, and they made musical instruments, tools, hunting gear and jewelry. They even had a hyoid bone identical to ours which means that they could talk. The only honest conclusion is that Neanderthal Man was human.

Because of the overwhelming secular bias, which has undermined scientific research and education since the late 1800s, such information is not widely announced. Sadly, most people still think Neanderthal Man refutes the Bible.

Again, beware of science falsely so called. Speaking of which, let's review Lucy. *Australopithecus Afarensis* (pithecus means ape) was discovered in Ethiopia in 1974. Lucy has been the messiah for Darwinism ever since. [60]

Supposed proof that Lucy was a link between ape and man included that she walked in an upright manner and that her thighbone (femur) angled to the knee, as do human thighbones. However, in 1987 it was reported: *Anatomists have concluded these creatures are not a link between ape and man, and did not walk upright in the human manner.* [61] Other discoveries include that most tree-dwelling apes have femurs that angle to the knee.

Also, other Australopithecus Afarensis fossils reveal they had curved toes and fingers so they could grab hold of tree limbs. The fact is that Lucy was just an ape that provides no viable evidence for Darwinism in action. Still, Lucy adorns textbooks today, usually presented as if walking upright like a person.62

The bottom line is that people need to distinguish scientific facts from secular-biased interpretations of the evidences, and beware of science falsely so called.

Modern textbooks also claim that two new hominids have been unearthed: Tomei Man and Flat Faced Man.

During 2001, a small ape skull was found that was crushed into about 50 pieces. After reconstructing the fragments it was announced that the face was *slightly* flatter than a normal ape's face and thus was born Flat Faced Man *(Kenyanthropus platyops)*.63 That was all it took for desperate Darwinists to put it into secular schoolbooks.64 What I have not read in the secular textbooks is that Flat Faced Man stood about three-feet tall!

Tomei man *(Sahelanthropus)* was found in 2002. The October 2002 edition of *Science News* reported: *The specimen's teeth resemble...ape lineages...it didn't walk on two legs...* 65 *Nature* reported in the same month that Tomei Man...*represents an ancient ape.* 66 Yet textbooks falsely claim Tomei Man is...*older than any hominid previously known.* 67

In May 2009, headlines around the world heralded the arrival of Ida: *The search for a direct connection between humans and the rest of the animal kingdom has taken 200 years - but it was presented to the world today...this transitional species finally confirms Charles Darwin's theory of evolution...*68

While the headlines made it sound as though Ida was a new find, she was actually discovered in 1983. *Fox News* reported: *The small body represents a roughly 9-month-old female that probably looked a lot like modern lemurs.* So Ida was actually a species of long-tailed primates that are found in zoos today.

Well, *there is not much pride when you're trapped inside a slowly sinking ship*, and by the end of 2009 Darwinian evangelists, in a special release of *Science*, announced *Ardipithecus ramidus* as another proof of Darwinism. Secular-biased scientists even

101

described Ardi as being more important than *Lucy* in the history of human evolution. Well, I have already discussed *Lucy* so let's review the facts about Ardi.

The *crushed bones* of about 40 apes were found in Ethiopia eighteen years before Ardi was announced to the world. *National Geographic News* reported that the bones were in such poor condition that they would turn to dust if touched.[69] It was from a mixture of these bones that Ardi was eventually constructed.

Honest scientists reported that Ardi is no more of a link between ape and man than are the many other refuted Darwinian claims. Anatomist William Jungers of Stonybrook stated, "Divergent big toes are associated with grasping, and this has one of the most divergent big toes you can imagine." NGN

Neanderthal Man, Lucy, Tomei Man, Flat Faced Man, Ida and Ardi will eventually join Java Man, Piltdown Man, Nebraska Man, Peking Man, Orce Man, and Ramipithecus on the list of infamous Darwinian ape men that have misled billions of people. [70]

This leaves me with a couple of observations and two questions: With hundreds of various types of apes and monkeys in the world today and with millions of individual primates having lived and died during the past 500 years, why does finding a monkey bone prove Darwinism? Doesn't it just prove that when monkeys die they leave their bones behind?

The truth is that the vaunted common ancestor only exists in the minds of the Darwinian faithful. *Discovery News* reported: *The last common ancestor of chimpanzees and humans remains a holy grail in science.*[71] Darwinism predicted science would provide plenty of fossil evidence showing that primates evolved into humans. Darwinism fails its own key criterion yet again.

The biblical view is that God created man in His own image on the sixth day of the week-long Creation; therefore, no viable evidence will be found of man having evolved from a primate. As of this writing, the observable science supports the Bible.

"Russ, I heard your '50 Facts versus Darwinism in the Textbooks.' I graduated with a BA in Physical Anthropology. My senior thesis 'Anterior Tooth Reductions in Ramapithecus' was published in 1970 in the Journal Primates. I eventually got a PhD and was a Professor at the University of Arizona. I once shared the lectern at a national conference with Stephen Gould. In other words I've been there done that! This is to say that you do a marvelous job with your presentations."

Dr. Yulish in AZ

Chapter Twelve

A Plethora of Misinformation

We all tend to look at things through our own bias. The difference is most of us do not put our unfounded biases into schoolbooks and teach them as if they were scientific facts.

Russ Miller

Have you ever done something that was really dumb? I have. And so have Darwinists who tend to assume that things which are not understood are proof for Darwinism. Their conclusions usually end up embarrassing them.

Junk DNA

Because *billions of years leading to Darwinism* never took place, Darwinists are left without any true examples to show of such change having occurred. Unfortunately, this fact does not prevent them from filling schoolbooks with an abundance of misinterpreted evidences.

For example, for the past half century Darwinists have been grossly misinterpreting that large portions of human DNA—portions whose function we did not understand—were Junk DNA left over from our Darwinian past. However, research is now showing that Junk DNA is not junk left over from our supposed evolutionary past, but instead likely holds the key to the entire RNA/DNA system!

Yet biology students from the 1950's through 2012 were taught Junk DNA proved we evolved over long ages without God.

The teaching of unfounded Darwinian bias in science classes is bad enough. What is even worse is that such erroneous teachings often continue to remain in schoolbooks and classrooms long after scientific scrutiny has proven the Darwinian conclusion to be in error. This is pure deception and is why it is vital to distinguish the difference between observable facts and Darwinian-biased interpretations of those facts.

Let's take a look at a few more deceptive examples employed to promote Darwinism.

Resistance to poisons

Darwinists teach that bugs becoming resistant to pesticides are proof for Darwinism. While examples of such resistance can be found, tests reveal they have nothing to do with new and beneficial genetic information being added to a gene pool. [72]

Mutations are caused by the mix-up or loss of the parents' genetic information (Gene Depletion). If not immediately fatal, mutations are generally neutral, or in rare cases, cause micro-changes within the victim of the mutation. They don't add new and beneficial genetic data (see Chapter nine) that eventually leads to Darwinian macro-evolution. [73]

In theory, resistance to a poison can occur due to a mutational loss of genetic information. For instance, if a mutation leads to a genetic loss that results in a genetic trait not being exhibited in the mutant, and if this trait is what the pesticide attacks in the mutant's siblings, the mutated insect may benefit from the loss and be resistant to that pesticide.

If the mutation is in a reproduction gene and is passed to its offspring, then the offspring will also be immune to the insecticide. However, this does not have anything to do with the macro-evolution of new kinds of insects. The bugs are still the same kind of insects as their ancestors, though they are now resistant to the particular insecticide.

These micro-changes will not lead to Darwinian macro-evolution. [74]

Bacteria and Viruses resistant to treatments

Observable scientific research shows that both bacteria and viruses, which reproduce quickly, accumulate mutations in their gene pools. Darwinists teach that bacteria and viruses becoming resistant to antibiotics is proof of Darwinian evolution. However, this is quite similar to bugs becoming resistant to insecticides.

One example Darwinists often cite is when a mutation allows an anti-penicillin enzyme to mass produce. However, this is caused by losing the ability to turn off the production of the enzyme, and it does not provide an overall beneficial change. Think about it. If the mutated bacterium were in a patient who was receiving penicillin, then the mutation would have provided that bacteria with a benefit. However, anywhere else, the genetically weaker mutant would be using up its energy producing the unneeded anti-penicillin enzyme. This would weaken the bacterium and tend to lead to its removal by Natural Selection. [75]

Even though bacteria becoming resistant to antibiotics have nothing to do with Darwinian change, many teacher guides instruct unsuspecting educators to teach their students that mutations create bacteria that are resistant to antibiotics, leading to Neo-Darwinian evolution. [76]

Darwinists also claim that mutations can cause viruses to evolve so they are resistant to known medical treatments. So, what does observable science reveal?

The facts reveal that viral treatments are made to recognize the shape, attach to, and then destroy a specific protein on a virus. Because of this, if a genetic loss due to a mutation alters the shape of the targeted protein, it could cause the protein to become unrecognizable to the antibiotic. In such a case, this loss of information would make the antibiotic useless.[77]

Once again, these are examples of losing genetic information and have nothing to do with the addition of new and beneficial genetic data. Losing information will not lead to the Neo-Darwinian evolution of new kinds of creatures.

So why don't Darwinists get rid of the misleading examples and simply present the real evidence of Darwinism in action? They don't have any because Darwinism is a scientific impossibility.

Pseudogenes

Darwinists often claim we have *shared mistakes* in our DNA with those found in the DNA of primates. Darwinists claim these errors accumulated during the unobserved period of time in which they believe primates were evolving into humans. These shared mistakes are referred to as pseudogenes. Any Darwinian hope in this biased interpretation fell apart when real science observed human and guinea pig pseudogenes share about 36% of the same mistakes. Since Darwinists do not believe we are closely related to guinea pigs, this logically refutes the claim that *shared mistakes* are proof of Darwinian evolution. Unfortunately, pseudogenes are still often used as proof that humans evolved from primates.[78]

ERVs

Endogenous (splicing) Retro (backwards copying) Viruses, ERVs for short, are another claimed proof that humans evolved from a primate ancestor.

Darwinists believe that sometime in the unobserved past a retrovirus injected a small strand of RNA into a cell. Then they think the strand of RNA spliced and copied itself backward into the cell's genetic data pertaining to reproduction. Since that time, Darwinists assume it has been passed from generation to generation. By assuming an ERV will always show up in the same place in the DNA strand, Darwinists search for an ERV in a chimp's DNA that is located in the same place as in the human's gene strand. Any such ERVs are claimed to be proof that we share a common ancestor with chimpanzees.

However, recent research has discovered that ERVs can move along the DNA strand. This finding refutes the claim that ERVs found in similar locations are proof of common ancestry.

I expect that real science will eventually find that ERVs, like supposed Junk DNA, were there from the start and play an important role in the overall RNA/DNA system.

Human Chromosome 2

Chromosomes hold genetic information. People have 46 chromosomes while apes have 48. To explain this discrepancy, Darwinists dig deep into their imaginations and claim this actually proves humans evolved from primates. How so?

Here is the story:
Telomeres are located at the end of all chromosomes. Because Darwinists believe we evolved from primates, they point to a telomere found within Human Chromosome 2 and claim it as proof two chromosomes fused together *in yet another unobserved primate ancestor* to form Human Chromosome 2.

Ignored is the fact that telomeres are often found within the genetic information contained inside of the chromosomes. In fact, more than ten other telomeres are found at other locations within Human Chromosome 2. This fact is ignored by those promoting Darwinism.

Had there been a fusion of two primate chromosomes, the DNA sequences on both sides of the alleged fusion in Human Chromosome 2 would be similar to a chimp's genetic sequences. However, studies reveal the sequences are quite different. Human Chromosome 2 contains complex genetic data that is not found in a primate's DNA. It is this genetic information that codes for the differences between an ape and a human. [79] Thus the genetic information is the key, not the number of chromosomes holding the data.

After all, tobacco plants, like apes, have 48 chromosomes, yet no one is claiming they are twins!

A fair question is, had such a fusion occurred, how did the primate sperm with 24 chromosomes fertilize an egg carrier that only had 23 chromosomes? Since they would not have matched up, we should have expected extinction of the creature with the fused chromosome.

The bottom line is that if Human Chromosome 2 were the result of a fusion, it would have been the fusion of two human chromosomes, not a fusion in some unknown primate *millions of years* ago.

The simple truth is that Human Chromosome 2 does not provide viable proof for Darwinism.

Recapitulation

Ernst Haeckel was one of the earliest of the Darwinian pioneers when it came to drawing things that never existed to promote their theory that never took place.

Haeckel read Darwin's book, but by 1869, ten years after the book was published, Haeckel had the same problem that Darwinists have today; he couldn't find any evidence to support Darwinism. So Haeckel did what Darwinists are famous for doing. He intelligently designed some fraudulent evidence. [80]

Haeckel drew a human in the embryonic stage and drew copies of the human with slight changes to each drawing. Next, he labeled his drawings as a human, chicken, salamander, fish, etc., all looking nearly identical. Then he claimed *ontogeny recapitulates phylogeny*! What that means is that creatures, including humans, go through their past evolutionary forms while they are still in their mother's womb. Though this was a fraud from the start, it became known as the Biogenetic Law or the Theory of Recapitulation.

Embryologist Dr. Michael Richardson stated, "What he (Haeckel) did was to take a human embryo and copy it...these are fakes". [81]

Haeckel's drawings were proven to be fraudulent in the 1870s yet variations are still often claimed as proof for common ancestry in colleges today. For instance, Darwinists show drawings of a human in the embryonic stage and claim that they have gill pouches from our past evolutionary stages. Real science has long proven that these were never gill pouches. They are simply areas that later develop into the organs in our throat. 82

With regard to dishonest Darwinists, the fact is that fraud in the 19th century is still fraud in the 21st century.

Though it often takes many years, real science eventually refutes the misinterpretations based on the erroneous belief in *goo to the zoo to you* Darwinian evolutionism.

When it comes to the plethora of claimed proofs of Darwinism, the bottom line is that people must be careful to distinguish facts from Darwinian-biased fantasies which have undermined scientific education.

Operational and historical science

Operational science and *historical science* are two categories of scientific research of which a person needs to be aware.

Operational science develops knowledge from the observation, study and repeatable testing of existing evidence. Operational science has led to many great improvements in our lifestyles, from radios to penicillin to iPods.

Historical science takes present-day findings and applies them to events that occurred in the past, events that cannot be observed in the present. A large portion of both geology and biology are historical sciences.

I often say that real science is a Believer's best friend. What I am actually trying to convey is that things that can be observed support the Word of God when they are correctly interpreted.

A scientific hypothesis must be realistic in nature, predictable, testable, and refutable.

True theories come from hypotheses which are built upon evidence. Darwin based his hypothesis on micro-adaptations, such as finches bringing forth finches with slight variations. Then, without any evidence of macro-evolution, he postulated that micro-adaptations within species would be found to lead to macro-changes where a finch would evolve into something other than a finch.

Darwinism predicted biology would find proof that higher life forms have evolved from lower life forms. This would be reliable, empirical criteria supporting Darwinism.

Darwinism consistently fails its own key criterion.

The failed predictions would refute Darwinism if it were true science. However, it lives on because it is a religious belief which, combined with a belief in *billions of years* of time, provides the foundation for modern Naturalism and Humanism.

I was surprised by the lack of viable evidence in support of *billions of years* or Darwinism. Before long I realized that **billions of years, Darwinism, Naturalism and Humanism are religious beliefs that have a symbiotic relationship**, a term generally applied to plants or animals. A symbiotic relationship is where one, or both, entities have a dependence on the other to survive. Though a belief in *billions of years* can exist without Darwinism, Naturalism or Humanism, a belief in Darwinism, Naturalism or Humanism cannot survive without *billions of years* of time.

Humanists own the educational and scientific establishments. They *appeal to the unknown* by arguing that unless every conceivable possibility to support their beliefs can be proven impossible, no matter how improbable (aliens may have dropped us off), only their philosophy can be considered. In essence, they force all opposing views to prove a negative, which is impossible. This makes *billions of years leading to Darwinism* non-refutable.

111

Since Darwinism fails its own predictions and has been made to be non-refutable, Darwinism qualifies as a religious belief.

As the evidence against Darwinism continues to mount, look for more false claims and far-fetched stories to try to camouflage its collapse. Philosopher Malcolm Muggeridge stated, "...the theory of evolution...will be one of the great jokes in the history books of the future. Posterity will marvel that so flimsy and dubious an hypothesis could be accepted..." [83]

It is little wonder that Darwinism is the only *scientific theory* that requires legal rulings to keep it afloat. Darwin stated, "A fair result can be obtained only by fully stating and balancing the facts and arguments on both sides of each question." [84] It is long past due that Darwinian dogma be compared with observable facts as well as with viable competing hypotheses.

*"I lost my faith in college. As a senior Biology major I attended a talk you gave on my campus. It made me mad at you for challenging what I had been taught. In fact, I was livid! Two years later I was teaching Darwinism in a public school and you spoke at my parent's church. I attended to hear what nonsense you would share but before your sermon ended I humbled myself to the Truth of God and His Word. **I now teach Creation-based science in a Christian school.**"*

Anonymous in AZ

"I am a Biology major. Today the professor gave the example of gill slits in a baby while in the mother's womb, which you had shown were simply folds in the skin which later develop into organs in the throat area. I just want to thank you for what you are doing. God bless."

Jesse in OR

Reprove not a scorner, lest he hate thee; rebuke a wise man, and he will love thee. Proverbs 9:8

Chapter Thirteen

A Plethora of Evil Fruit

Wherefore by their fruits ye shall know them.
Lord Jesus the Christ in Matthew 7:20

Have you ever pondered some of the issues pertaining to *billions of years leading to Darwinism*?

I spent the previous six chapters going over the top ten predictions of what I consider to be the Number One Evil Fruit coming from the tree of old-earth beliefs: Darwinism. In this chapter, I want to take a look at seven more of the *Top Ten Evil Fruits of Old-Earth Beliefs*. The truth is that *billions of years* and Darwinism have combined to allow these evil fruits to flourish.

Naturalism and Humanism

Billions of years leading to Darwinism has provided the philosophical foundation that has allowed both Naturalism and Secular Humanism to thrive.

Naturalism is a worldview that is based on a belief in materialistic atheism. It rejects all supernatural explanations of nature and holds that the natural sciences are the sole basis of what can be known. This is also referred to as Philosophical Naturalism.

Secular Humanism, also referred to as Humanism, is a worldview founded upon Naturalism. Humanism rejects any belief in a supernatural cause being the basis of morality or decision making.

Both Naturalism and Humanism posit that humans are a part of nature, the same as a tree or an ant.

Humanists understand the importance of indoctrinating the masses in their worldview. Anthony Lewis, Pulitzer Prize-winning columnist for the *New York Times*, wrote an article during December of 2001, just three months after terrorists murdered thousands of innocent people and destroyed the World Trade Center Buildings in New York City. He stated that *fundamentalism menaces the peace*. Lewis went on to warn that fundamentalism *is not found in Islam alone* and compared such terrorism to Christians who believe in Creation and dare to question Darwin.

The biblical view is: ***Beware lest any man spoil you through philosophy...*** Colossians 2:8

Eugenics

If ranchers can selectively breed cattle to bring about better milk-producing cows, and if humans are just evolving animals, why not selectively breed people to improve our species? If you think that sounds too far-fetched to occur, think again.

The field of trying to "improve" the physical and mental characteristics of the human race is referred to as eugenics. Sir Francis Galton, who was Charles Darwin's cousin, is known as the Father of Eugenics. [85]

The word *eugenics* is made from a combination of Greek words which mean *well-born* and, on the surface, appears to be a fine endeavor. Unfortunately, history shows that the pursuit of eugenics has led to the premature death of millions of people in order to eliminate *unworthy gene pools* in order to improve the physical and mental characteristics of future generations.

Unethical eugenicists have cleansed whomever they decided are the unworthy gene pools through sterilization programs, abortion, infanticide, euthanasia, genocide, ethnic wars and promotion of the homosexual lifestyle.

After the Nazis put the practice of eugenics into practical use during World War II, the term became a dirty word. *The Annals of Eugenics* changed its name to the *Annals of Human Genetics;*

Eugenics Quarterly became known as the *Journal of Social Biology.* 86

As proof that if we do not learn from history we will repeat it, eugenics is back in vogue on college campuses, and in political discussions, around the world today.

The biblical view is *God created man in his own image, male and female.* Genesis 1:27

Politics is biology applied

The idea that *billions of years leading to Darwinism* resulted in human beings has been wholeheartedly embraced by those in political power who desire to impose themselves on others.

The belief that *Politics is biology applied* is directly founded on a belief in *billions of years leading to Darwinism.*

Nazism was certainly an example of *Politics is biology applied.* Ernst Haeckel, inventor of the fraudulent *Theory of Recapitulation* (Chapter 12), had a tremendous influence on German thought.

Adolph Hitler believed the Germans were the most evolved, superior race and deserved to rule the world. Besides the World War they started, the Nazi regime murdered 13 million people in their concentration camps. During 1971, the Scientific Origins of National Socialism claimed: *Social Darwinism...reached its peak in Nazi Germany under Hitler...the supreme evolutionist and Nazism the ultimate fruit of the evolutionary tree.* 87 But they were wrong about Hitler being the ultimate fruit.

The biblical view is some people are, *Ever learning, and never able to come to the knowledge of the truth...men of corrupt minds, reprobate concerning the faith.* 2 Timothy 3:7-8

Karl Marx is often referred to as the Father of Communism. During the 1800's he was a philosopher and political activist. He wrote the *Communist Manifesto* (1848) and *Das Kapital* (1867).

Marx welcomed *billions of years leading to Darwinism* as such beliefs helped to rid society of God and His inherent morals. Any political philosophy, such as communism, which has led to the death of millions of its own citizens, certainly qualifies as an example of *Politics is biology applied.*

Marxism itself is an economic and sociopolitical worldview. Marxism posits that a classless system, based on common ownership of production abilities and services, will evolve better and better until it becomes a perfect utopia with economic abundance and freedom for individuals to develop their talents. In reality, such a godless system always fails since it does not account for mankind's sinful nature (the laziness of some; the greed for power and wealth by others).

Marx is quoted as having said, **"My object in life is to dethrone God and destroy capitalism."**

The biblical view is ***evil men and seducers shall wax worse and worse.*** 2 Timothy 3:13

Marxist dictator Mao Tse-Tung believed that *Politics is biology applied.* He murdered 60 million people in China from 1949 into the 1970's and listed Charles Darwin as his favorite author.[88]

Marx's *Communist Manifesto* included having the government provide free education for children in public schools.

Horace Mann was the first Chairman of America's public school system and is revered as the Father of Public Education. He said, "We who are engaged in the sacred cause of education are entitled to look upon all parents as having given hostages to our cause."

John Dewey (1859-1952) was a psychologist, political activist, educational reformer and the first president of the American Humanist Association, the largest atheist organization in America. He was also one of the 34 signers of the original

Humanist Manifesto (1933) which is founded on *billions of years leading to Darwinian evolution.* He was enormously influential in America's public education system and promoted Progressive Education, which now dominates public school teaching in the USA.

Creation and prayer removed from America's schools

Did you know that through 1962 American schools taught from the Bible? Biblical Creation was often taught and prayers were given daily to the God of Scripture. However, during 1963, prayer and biblical Creation (the foundation for both the Gospel and for America's freedoms – the Declaration of Independence: *All men are **created** equal and endowed by their **Creator** with certain unalienable rights*) was removed from America's public schools and replaced by *billions of years leading to Darwinism* (the foundation for Humanism). I will discuss how and why this occurred in the next chapter.

Hitler and Marx understood the importance of indoctrinating the youth in their worldview. They understood that whoever controlled the textbooks would control the state.

Humanists understand this as well, and since 1963 textbooks have taught unsuspecting children it is *a fact that life on Earth has evolved and that organisms have changed over billions of years.*89

In 1962, the U.S.A.'s public schools were highly rated around the world in math, science and in overall education. Today, America's schools rank in the bottom twenty percent worldwide.

During 1962, the top public school issues were kids talking out of turn and chewing gum in class. Today's problems include alcohol abuse, drug use, gang rape, pregnancy, abortion, suicide, and mass murder.

We are to tell good from bad by the fruit.

The Moral Collapse of American Society and Moral Relativism

By 1965, the Drug Culture and the Sexual Revolution exploded across the countryside. At that time there were only two primary sexually transmitted diseases. Today there are about sixty, including the AIDS virus.

By the late 1960s, many of the radical groups which have greatly contributed to the undermining of the moral foundations on which American society had been built, began to sprout from the tree of *billions of years leading to Darwinism.*

These included radical environmental groups, the women's liberation movement, alternative lifestyle groups, and radical animal rights organizations.

Peter Singer, known as the Father of the Animal Rights Movement, stated, "Christianity is our foe. If animal rights is to succeed, we must destroy the Judeo-Christian religious tradition."

The 2006 Distinguished Texas Scientist, per the Texas Academy of Science, was a University of Texas professor who said the deaths of 5.8 billion people are needed to keep Earth from turning into *a fat, human biomass.*

Wild Earth, a radical environmental paper, stated: *the extinction of Homo Sapiens ...phasing out the human race will solve every problem on earth, social and environmental.* [90] I suppose that the extinction of human beings would clear up every social issue.

The biblical view is there will be those *who changed the truth of God into a lie, and worshipped and served the creature more than the Creator.* Romans 1:25

Moral Relativism

The belief that we came about over long ages of evolutionary processes led to the acceptance there is no God to provide us with moral guidelines. This opened the door for moral relativism which is a philosophical view that there are no absolute truths. What may be right or wrong is up to each person, each individual circumstance, and what society will accept.

To say there is anything wrong with abortion, pornography (the USA is now the world's leading exporter of porn), same-sex marriage, witchcraft or Satanism (paganism is doubling every 18 months in the USA) [95] would lead to being called mean, judgmental, arrogant and unloving.

Name-calling is the last bastion for those with no evidence to back up their position. Saul Alinsky would be proud.

Rules for Radicals

During 1971, Neo-Marxist Saul Alinsky's *Rules for Radicals* was published. Alinsky, who is known as the Original Community Organizer, based his rules for changing a nation on the tactics of Italian Neo-Marxist Antonio Gramsci.

Neo-Marxism is a loose term for various approaches that try to answer questions that were not covered in the writings of Karl Marx.

In his book's opening dedication. Alinsky acknowledged Lucifer as the very first radical *who rebelled against the establishment.* [91]

The two primary goals of *Rules for Radicals* are to undermine both biblical absolutes and Christian morals in a culture in order to cause the society to implode upon itself.

Harry Truman said, "The fundamental basis of this nation's law was given to Moses on the Mount... If we don't have the proper moral background, we will finally end up with a totalitarian government." [92]

Alinsky stated, "The first step in community organization is community disorganization." His rules reflect this, as rule number one is to cause conflict in order to divide people into opposing groups that are hostile to one another. He suggested a Community Organizer would first create conflict to divide people by their race, religion, income, gender, etc.

Because most people do not like conflict, they naturally flow toward the second rule which is to compromise. Since the groups previously held a position, the compromise is always away from their initial principles and toward the radical position.

Rule number three deals with those who stand on their principles and refuse to compromise. Such people are, according to the third rule, to be marginalized. Alinsky suggested that ridicule is the radical's most potent weapon. By calling the opposition names, such as racist, fundamentalist, stupid, unloving, mean-spirited, arrogant, etc. they would get others to distance themselves from them. We certainly can observe these rules throughout American society today.

Abortion

Because of the belief that humans are just evolving animals, in 1973 abortion was legalized in the United States.

Note: Whenever I mention abortion I feel I need to address the fact that many Christian women have had abortions. If you are one of these women, know that God loves you and that He sent His only begotten Son to pay for all of our sins. So make sure you ask God to forgive you (He will instantaneously). Then be sure to forgive yourself by fully accepting God's grace.

Now a message for men (because we can be a bit dense at times): If a woman has had an abortion, a man has had one as well. If this applies to you, make sure you ask God to forgive you. He will.

As of this writing 55+ million American citizens have been killed. Worldwide more than 2 billion defenseless babies have been slaughtered. But even abortion is not the *ultimate fruit of the evolutionary tree.*

Margaret Sanger founded Planned Parenthood in 1916 to eliminate what she called *human weeds* and inferior races like

Orientals, Jews and Blacks. [93] Sanger, a noted promoter of eugenics, said that she looked forward to seeing humanity free *of the tyranny of Christianity* (which posits humans are made in the image of God, so you cannot kill off those you deem unfit to live). [94]

These are but a few of the evil fruits found hanging from the branches of the corrupted tree of *billions of years leading to Darwinism.* I discussed the number one fruit, Darwinism, in the preceding chapters. I have saved the *ultimate fruit* for chapter 15 but first let's discuss the loss of America's Christian heritage in the next chapter.

"As a professional Chemist, I recommend Russ Miller to you. Russ has worked diligently to gather and organize compelling presentations of scientific evidence in support of God's creation, which he relates to scripture. These seminars strongly support that God created the universe and all life."

Dr. Jack Swenson,
Former Chemistry Dept. Chairman,
Northern Arizona University

Chapter Fourteen

The Theft of America's Heritage

Whenever the pillars of Christianity shall be over thrown, our present republican forms of government...must fall with them. Founding Father, Dr. Jedidiah Morse

To destroy the United States of America an enemy must accomplish two things. First, destroy the citizens' faith in the Bible's foundational teachings, the **COSt**. Second, rewrite America's great history.

It is a straight forward plan which requires consistent effort and a lot of patience, and many people have been striving to implement it for the past 200 years.

Think about it. Undermine people's faith in there being a loving Creator with whom we need to be reconciled, the foundation of the Gospel message, and you also destroy people's belief that there is a Creator who endowed them with their rights.

The strategy is deviously brilliant in its simplicity.

Tear down the citizenry's trust in the biblical foundations, then rewrite the history of the United States, and we *the people* will soon forget that our rights were endowed to us by our Creator. By erasing the country's Christian heritage and downplaying the nation's true past, *we the people* may not see any reason to stand up for what we have inherited. As a result, we may allow America's unalienable freedoms to be rewritten or removed by governmental bureaucrats; just as most of America's great Christian heritage has been removed.

The primary attack upon the history of the United States has been focused on the Provider of the country's freedoms. It was evident to America's adversaries that to destroy the USA, they had to undermine faith in the God of the Bible within the heart and mind of the average American citizen. Realizing this, the enemy centered their crosshairs on the **COS†**.

I cannot overstress the importance, for anyone seeking the truth, of understanding the relationship between the early chapters of the book of Genesis, the Gospel of the Lord Jesus, and America's freedoms. Only with this knowledge can a person grasp how an attack on Christianity is an attack on America's Creator-given rights.

Many generations of dedicated Humanists have devoted their lives and resources to gain the stranglehold they now have on public education in the USA. To read most of today's Humanistic textbooks, or to hear a history lesson provided by the majority of secular college professors, one would walk away thinking Christianity had little, if anything, to do with the founding of America and that the biblical God had nothing to do with the achievements the nation has enjoyed.

Humanists have indoctrinated U.S. citizens by the millions into believing a litany of lies which include: their nation was not founded on predominantly Christian principles; their Constitution is a living (changeable) document; most of the Founders were not Christians; the Founding Fathers were evil capitalists and horrible slave owners; humans evolved over long ages of time; and God has no place in public schools or government institutions.

Karl Marx, the Father of Communism, believed the way to revolutionary takeover of a nation was to destroy the culture's knowledge of its heritage. He knew that people without a heritage are easily misled and thus understood the first battlefield was the rewriting of a country's history.

Marx is quoted as having said: "The first requisite for the happiness of the people is the abolition of religion." The Father of Communism's ideas did not fall on deaf ears.

In the late 1800's Dr. A.A. Hodge of Princeton predicted "...a centralized system of national education...will prove the most appalling enginery for the propagation of anti-Christian and atheistic unbelief..."

Over the past 40 years the USA's history has been rewritten or ignored. America's schoolchildren have been, and are, growing up with little knowledge of their nation's Christian roots. Historical revisionists, especially those holding positions as textbook authors and publishers, not only deny, or embarrass children about, America's Judeo-Christian heritage but they also teach students to be ashamed of their country's Founding Fathers.

Houghton Mifflin Harcourt's *Social Studies*, Teachers Edition, 1994 reads, "When Jefferson wrote 'all men' are equal, he really meant 'all citizens' - women and blacks were not included." This is simply anti-American propaganda as the context of the Declaration of Independence makes clear the term "men" refers to all mankind.

Here is an example of a role playing exercise for students from *Discover Our Heritage*, Teachers Edition (Boston: Houghton Mifflin), 1997: *Take the role of a Roman disturbed by the rise of Christianity, and write a letter explaining why you are opposed to Christianity.*

How do you suppose this type of propaganda, found in a child's public school textbook, impacts an impressionable young mind?

It is ironic that people from around the world often risk everything to have the opportunity to live in the *Land of the Free*, yet youth in America are being taught to be embarrassed and ashamed of their country's past. And the nation's public educational system combines these types of messages with telling children they evolved over *billions of years* of time without God.

I saw a reporter on FOX News ask high school graduates if they would be willing to fight to save the USA. The answers were generally, "What for?" or "No way!"

The lack of appreciation for the country the students are inheriting, often times reaching the level of disdain, has been achieved through the rewriting of the nation's history coupled with the anti-American and anti-Christian propaganda promoted in America's public school textbooks. Their true heritage has been stolen from them and from future generations of Americans, and people without a heritage are easily persuaded.

My people are destroyed for a lack of knowledge. Hosea 4:6

In order to understand what citizens of the United States have lost, and stand to lose, we need to review where we began and what we were given.

The fact that America's true history has been stolen began to become apparent to me during an excursion with my wife, Joanna, to Washington, D.C. during March of 2007.

While visiting our nation's capital we were blown away by the paintings and drawings in the National Art Museum. The majority of artwork from the early history of the United States contained a biblical theme.

After leaving the museum we were truly mesmerized as we visited various federal institutions and memorials in the nation's capitol. At many of these sites we found quotes etched into the stone walls proclaiming belief and/or gratitude to the biblical God from some of the nation's Founding Fathers. We also found depictions of the Ten Commandments, Bible verses and testimonials inscribed in brass and carved into marble or granite, each attesting to America's once powerful faith in, and reliance on, the God of the Christian Bible.

The truth is that it is difficult to visit America's capitol without concluding the nation was founded by predominantly Christian men and women on predominantly Christian principles, and that faith in the biblical Creator had a significant impact on the course of the nation's history. Yet, without knowledge of their true past, American citizens can be led to believe whatever the powers that be place before them.

For we wrestle not against flesh and blood, but against principalities, against powers, against the rulers of the darkness of this world, against spiritual wickedness in high places. Ephesians 6:12

It is essential for Americans to be aware of the facts that God created all men equal and gifted them their rights which mankind, or man-made entities, cannot take from them. The nation's foes realize this and know that to destroy the USA they must wipe out the citizens' faith in their Creator, for if there was not a Creator, there are not any Creator-given rights.

Fingerprints of God

The fingerprint of God was upon the hearts of the early discoverers and settlers who set sail for America. These included Christopher Columbus, the Puritans and the Pilgrims. Even most universities, such as Yale and Harvard, began as Christian institutions.

The First Great Awakening

Yet by the early 1700's both the Christian Church and the people of the Thirteen Colonies had lost their zeal for the true biblical God. Likewise, most universities had succumbed to the allure of secular compromise (as have most of today's Christian institutions as I discuss in my book, *The Submerging Church*).

Then came the first *Great Awakening*, which was a 1732-1776 Christian revival that began in New England.

During this time, several God-honoring pastors, including Jonathan Edwards, returned to preaching "Christ died for you" from their pulpits. They were soon joined by British evangelist George Whitefield, preaching "Christ died for you" in town squares, fields and meadows where God poured forth His blessings and the crowds of people grew to the thousands.

As the first Great Awakening took off, other pastors returned to proclaiming "Christ died for you" and soon the Thirteen Colonies became bonded as *One nation under God.*

Creation-based worldview

It is vital to understand the Colonists held to a Creation-based worldview so they understood the **COS†**. Thus when people were told "Christ died for you" they understood why Christ was crucified and how His sacrifice on the cross would redeem Believers with their heavenly Creator.

In the early chapters of Acts 17 we learn that when the apostle Paul reasoned with Jews, who held to a Creation-based worldview, he began by declaring: **"Jesus, whom I preach unto you, is Christ."**

The Jews understood the need for their redemption because they knew God's perfect Creation had been corrupted by Adam's Original sin which Separated them from their loving Creator and required that they be † reconciled, with Him. They understood the Scriptural foundations. Because of this the apostle Paul did not need to explain to the Jews why they needed a Savior. He simply proclaimed to them that Jesus was the promised Messiah.

Likewise, the people living in the thirteen original colonies were aware of their need for redemption with their Creator so they could understand and accept that "Christ died for you." Once God poured forth His Holy Spirit the Great Awakening took off and the Thirteen Colonies demanded their God-given rights back from the British. These they secured through the Revolutionary War. In fact, the Liberty Bell is inscribed with:

"Proclaim Liberty throughout all the land unto all the inhabitants thereof." Leviticus 25:10

Writings and quotes from our Founding Fathers and sermons from Christian pastors leading up to the Revolutionary War attest to the fact that the United States of America was primarily built upon Christian principles, including the Ten Commandments, and that we were endowed by our biblical Creator with certain unalienable rights.

During a sermon in Charleston, Massachusetts on April 25, 1799, Founding Father Dr. Jedidiah Morse, a former divinity student at Yale, stated, "Whenever the pillars of Christianity shall be over thrown, our present republican forms of government...must fall with them."

Dr. Morse knew the freedoms American's enjoy were endowed to them from their Scriptural Creator. Because of this knowledge he understood that if the faith of *we the people* in the foundations of Christianity were undermined so would be our freedoms and the Republic's form of government.

Noah Webster (1758-1843) wrote the first American Dictionary and assembled the Blue Back Speller which was used to educate America's children at a time when America's youth were considered some of the best-educated children in the world.

Webster stated, "Our liberty, growth and prosperity were a result of a Biblical philosophy on life." He attested, "The Christian religion is...one of the first things in which all children...ought to be instructed."

Webster made these statements because he understood, as he said, "The Christian religion must be the basis of any government intended to secure the rights and privileges of a free people."

It is vital for all Americans, Christian and non-Christian alike, to understand the importance of the early chapters of the Book of Genesis to the freedoms they enjoy.

America's first Surgeon General, Founding Father Dr. Benjamin Rush, said, "The only foundation for...a Republic is to be laid in Religion...Christianity is the only true and perfect religion."

Only by understanding the relationship between the Jesus of Scripture, who is our Creator, and America's freedoms, can a person comprehend how an attack on Creation is an attack on the freedoms endowed by God to American citizens as described in the Declaration of Independence, and spelled out in the U.S. Constitution and its attached Bill of Rights.

While the Founding Fathers were predominantly men of strong faith, they were not perfect, just as there are no perfect men today. Only one perfect, sinless man has ever lived on earth, Jesus Christ who was 100% man and 100% God. Yet, of the Founding Fathers, fifty-two of the fifty-six signers of the Declaration of Independence (93%) and fifty-two of the fifty-five authors of the U.S. Constitution (95%) were Christians.

During the nation's formative, revolutionary war years, state constitutions had Christian Doctrines incorporated in them. Here are five examples.

Constitution of Delaware:
That every citizen who should be chosen a member of either house of the Legislature, or appointed to any other office, should be required to subscribe to the following declaration: *I do profess faith in God the Father, and in the Lord Jesus Christ his only son, and in the Holy Ghost, one God and blessed for evermore; and I do acknowledge the Holy Scriptures of the Old and New Testaments to be given by divine inspiration.*

Constitution of Massachusetts amended in 1780:
...the people of this commonwealth have the right to invest their legislature with power to authorize and require, and the legislature shall, from time to time, authorize and require, the several towns, parishes, precincts, and other bodies politic, or religious societies, to make suitable provision, at their own expense, for the institution of the public worship, and for the support and maintenance of public Protestant teachers of piety, Religion and morality... any chosen governor, lieutenant governor, senator or representative, and accepting the trust, shall subscribe a solemn profession that he believes in the Christian religion and has a firm persuasion of its truth.

Constitution of North Carolina included in 1776:

That no person who should deny the being of a God, or the truth of the Protestant religion, or the divine authority of either the Old or New Testament, or who should hold religious principles incompatible with the freedom and safety of the State, should be capable of holding any office or place of trust in the civil government of this State.

Constitution of Pennsylvania adopted in 1776:

(required of all legislative members declare): I do believe in one God, the Creator and Governor of the universe, the Rewarder of the good, and the Punisher of the wicked; and I acknowledge the Scriptures of the Old and New Testaments to be given by inspiration.

Constitution of South Carolina approved in 1778:

That all persons and religious societies who acknowledge there is one God, and a future state of rewards and punishments, and that God is to be publicly worshipped, shall be tolerated.

NOTE: These excerpts from state constitutions of the Revolutionary War years were taken from *The Christian Life and Character of The Civil Institutions of the United States* by Benjamin Morris. These were first published during the 1860's and republished during 2007 by American Vision, Inc.

America's Founding Fathers were men of extreme courage and conviction who put their lives and fortunes on the line by preparing, writing and signing the *Declaration of Independence*. This foundational document of the USA refers to the Biblical Creator as:

- **Provider of our rights** ("endowed by their creator")
- **Nature's Lawmaker** ("laws of nature; nature's God")
- **Supreme Judge** ("the Supreme Judge of the world")
- **Divine Protector** ("protection of Divine Providence")

John Hancock was the first signer of the *Declaration*. He led a

Congressional Proclamation on April 15, 1775 which attested to the Congress's desire: "...to humble themselves before God...to implore the Forgiveness of all our transgressions..." and asked for "...a Blessing on the...American Colonies in Defense of their Rights (for which we desire to thank Almighty God)..."

When Hancock penned his *John Hancock* to the world-changing Declaration on Independence Day, July 4, 1776, he also signed his death warrant should the British capture him. Most of the remaining 55 Founding Fathers signed the *Declaration* on August 2, 1776.

"...God created man in his own image...male and female..." Genesis 1:27

The Founding Fathers of the United States believed this biblical principle and declared in the Declaration: **"All men are created equal and endowed by their creator with certain unalienable rights..."** The Founding Fathers made clear that America's freedoms came from the Creator directly to its citizens.

Patrick Henry, the Orator of the Revolution, said the Bible: "...is a book worth more than all the other books ever printed."

George Washington, known as the Father of the Nation, wrote to his troops on July 2, 1776, while he was Commander of the Continental Army (in his General Orders): "The fate of unborn millions will now depend, under God, on the courage and conduct of this army."

Regardless of the true facts, here is an email I received from a victim of America's rewritten history: "It's a shame you don't know our history and you won't get away with your Christian lies! The U.S. Constitution is a secular document."

Since this is basically what is taught in the rewritten history of the USA, what do the facts reveal?

In the years following the Revolutionary War, the 13 original states began falling away from each other due to disagreements over various issues, including trade rights. As a result, a Constitutional Convention was convened in Philadelphia during May of 1787.

The three main reference sources for the U.S. Constitution, cited by the Constitution's authors themselves, were: *The King James Bible*; *The Commentaries On The Laws Of England* by Sir William Blackstone; and *The Spirit Of The Laws* by Baron Montesquieu.

These three sources reveal that the nation's *rule of law* was based on the never changing *natural law* of God's Ten Commandments.

Taken in the proper context, it is clear that the term *endowed by their creator,* penned into the Declaration, is the proper context through which we can correctly interpret both the U.S. Constitution and its attached Bill of Rights.

That the Founding Fathers believed in the biblical Creator and that America's freedoms came from God directly to the citizenry of the newly formed nation is seen in the opening sentence of the U.S. Constitution: **"We the people..."** rather than "We the government." It is abundantly clear that America's Founders believed each person's rights came from their biblical Creator.

During the Constitutional Convention, Ben Franklin, not known to have been a Christian at the time, proposed that each session should begin with a prayer to the God of the Bible and since 1787 every single session of Congress has begun with a prayer to the biblical God (until 2007 when a session of Congress opened with prayer to the god of Islam).

Following the Constitutional Convention, Alexander Hamilton, lead author of the *Federalist Papers* which interpreted the U.S. Constitution, and the USA's first Treasury Secretary said,
"I sincerely esteem (the Constitution) a system which, without the finger of God, never could have been...agreed upon by such a diversity of interests."

During President George Washington's inaugural address on April 30, 1789, he said, "No people can be bound to acknowledge and adore the Invisible Hand which conducts the affairs of men more than those of the United States..."

President Washington ended his oath by saying, **"So help me God"** as he bent down to kiss the Bible and he proclaimed a national Day of Thanksgiving to the Christian God on October 3, 1789. (The Thanksgiving proclamation presented by Abraham Lincoln is the one that is observed today).

In a letter sent to the Third Division of the Militia of Massachusetts on October 11, 1798 Founding Father John Adams, who became the second President of the United States, observed, "Our Constitution was made for a moral and religious people. It is wholly inadequate to the government of any other."

Founding Father Thomas Jefferson, known as the author of the Declaration of Independence, became the third U.S. President. Though rewritten history teaches he was a Christian skeptic and a Deist, in a letter to Founding Father Dr. Benjamin Rush on April 12, 1802, Jefferson wrote that his views were the, "...result of a life of inquiry and reflection, and much different from the anti-Christian system imputed to me by those who know nothing of my opinions."

President Jefferson attended Christian church services held in the U.S. Capital Building as well as in the building housing the Supreme Court. He also wrote the education plan for the District of Columbia schools employing the King James Bible as the primary reading book. From his actions and statements it is clear he wanted the USA built upon Christian principles.

James Madison, another of America's Founding Fathers, was known as the Father of the Bill of Rights. If anyone would have understood the *separation of church and state* it would have been this man who is also known to be the author of the First Amendment's religious clause.

Madison was elected as the fourth U.S. President and while in office he attended Christian church services that were held in the U.S. Capitol Building. He also promoted the hiring of federally salaried pastors for the House and the Senate.

So where does the Constitutional separation of church and state come from?

Not from the U.S. Constitution which contains no such language! I will discuss this issue later in this chapter. For now note that the First Amendment begins: **"Congress shall make no law respecting an establishment of religion, or prohibiting the free exercise thereof."**

The *religious clause* clearly prohibits the establishment of an official federal government religion yet leaves decisions regarding religious activities up to the discretion of the people of each individual state to decide upon for themselves.

From the Declaration of Independence to the U.S. Constitution to the Bill of Rights it is evident to any candid observer that the USA was predominantly founded on Christian principles and that the First Amendment's *religious clause* was intended to protect religious activities, not to undermine America's Christian-based freedoms.

Founding Father John Adams stated, "The general principles on which the fathers achieved independence were...the general principles of Christianity..."

From personal writings and the actions of many of America's Founding Fathers it is clear they intended to forge *One Nation Under God* that kept the federal government out of the church while ensuring that Christian principles would remain in the government.

Why so? So the U.S. government would not become corrupted like the administrations in Europe had become.

The fingerprint of God is seen upon the work of America's Founding Fathers and upon the nation they forged. The Founding Fathers are worthy of respect and admiration. Without their overall bond of faith in the biblical God, the United States of America never would have come into existence.

True history is never like a pristine story from a book of fairy tales. Real history involves real people who, like each of us, are sinful by the very nature we inherited from Adam and Eve.

The original Thirteen Colonies, though largely Christian-based, were not perfect either. Christians are only saved by God's grace through their faith in the Lord Jesus. They are not sinless and neither was the new nation founded by predominantly Christian citizens on predominantly biblical principles.

Slavery

The United States of America was founded at a time when slavery was commonplace around the world. In what was to become the USA, the African slave trade was thriving, especially in the plantation-oriented southern colonies. While America's rewritten history depicts our Founding Fathers as manipulating capitalists who often owned their own slaves, the true history reveals a different picture.

The Founding Fathers had several seemingly impossible tasks to overcome before the Thirteen Colonies could receive their God-given rights.

First, they needed to defeat the British Empire, the world's super power of the era. What slight chance they had of accomplishing this feat depended on their ability to unite all of the Thirteen Colonies in a long, expensive and deadly struggle, the Revolutionary War.

And the war for America's freedom and independence was very costly in both blood and treasure.

The nation's rewritten history is aimed at school children and designed to deprive Americans of their proud heritage. It makes innocent children ashamed of their brave and heroic Founders who in fact were highly educated, intelligent, and brave men who planted the seeds that led to the abolition of slavery in the USA.

The seeds of freedom were sown in the very Declaration of Independence where our Founding Fathers declared: **"All men are created equal and endowed by their creator with certain unalienable rights."** Though it took more than eighty years, a mighty Christian-led movement, and the sacrifice of hundreds of thousands of American lives to bear fruit, these words led to the abolition of slavery in America.

The Second Great Awakening

As the saying goes, if we do not learn from history we will repeat it, and man's desire to go his own way, against God's guidelines, began to corrupt America's culture.

By the late 1700's Europe's Age of Reason had invaded the United States. This was a collection of man-made philosophies which attempted to answer life's questions without God and once again the American people and the Christian Church lost touch with the true biblical God. But the people still held to a Creation-based view. This would once again play an important role in America's return to God's grace.

In 1795 Yale appointed Timothy Dwight as their new president and he began urging student's to use their God-given skills and abilities to serve God. Lyman Beecher was attending Yale at the time and became a pastor after his graduation.

During the 1820's Pastor Beecher began preaching, "Christ died for you" and the attendance at his church began to swell. Other pastors took note and returned to preaching "Christ died for you" from their pulpits as God poured forth His Holy Spirit and the second Great Awakening blanketed the nation which united again as *One nation under God.*

This Christian movement led the crusade to abolish slavery.

Have we not all one father? Hath not one God created us?

Malachi 2:10

John Quincy Adams, the sixth President of the United States, was a staunch anti-slavery advocate. During a speech he presented on Independence Day, 1837, President Adams rhetorically asked, "Is it not that the Declaration of Independence...laid the cornerstone of human government upon the precepts of Christianity?"

*And God said, Let us make man in our image, after our likeness...*Genesis 1:26a

Abraham Lincoln, the 16th president of the U.S., understood that America's freedoms came from the biblical Creator and *that all men were created equal.*

And hath made of one blood all nations of men for to dwell on all the face of the earth... Acts 17:26

The United States Secretary of State during the Lincoln administration was Anti-Slavery Activist William H. Seward who stated, "The whole hope of human progress is suspended on the ever growing influence of the Bible."

Though more than one single issue led to the discord, President Lincoln committed the nation to the Civil War, also known as the *War To Free The Slaves*, and relied on the power of Divine Providence to guide him through the horrible conflict.

While our rewritten history shames America's school children with the nation's involvement in the slave trade, kids are denied the fact that, though founded in a world full of slavery, American citizens chose to die to honor biblical principles which include:

Greater love hath no man than this, that a man lay down his life for his friends. John 15:13

In fact, the *Battle Hymn of the Republic* included the words: *"...as He died to make men holy let us die to make men free..."* And hundreds of thousands of America's young men died in the war to set all men free.

Returning to the fingerprints of God upon the history of America, a grateful nation erected a memorial to the *Father of the Nation.* The cornerstone to George Washington's Monument was laid down during 1848. Inside of it were placed a copy of the U.S. Constitution, the Declaration of Independence and the Bible.

Built and rebuilt between 1793 and 1858, the U.S. Capitol Building contains numerous references to America's Christian heritage. Christian-oriented engravings etched into the stone walls of the U.S. Capitol Building include *In God We Trust* and *America! God shed his grace on thee.*

Inside of the Capitol Building's Rotunda are eighteen foot wide paintings which include Pocahontas being baptized. This was hung in the Rotunda during 1840. Hung in 1844 is a painting of the Pilgrims praying for God's protection prior to setting sail to the New World, and a painting of the October 12, 1492 West Indies landing of Christopher Columbus has adorned the room since 1847. Columbus said: *"...it was the Lord who put it into my mind to sail to the new world."*

The Apotheosis of Washington beautifies the Rotunda's ceiling. This portrays George Washington's ascent into Heaven, surrounded by thirteen maidens representing the thirteen original Colonies.

Above the main door entering the House Chamber are the faces, carved in marble, of history's 23 greatest lawmakers. Eleven are seen to the left of the door and eleven to the right, all facing toward the front of the room where the Speaker of the House serves. Only the sides of their faces are seen. However, one special lawgiver is centered above the doorway so when the Speaker looks forward they can see the depiction of his entire face. This one individual is Moses, unto whom God gave the two tablets of stone, etched by the very finger of God, with the Ten

Commandments, on which the laws of the American nation were predominantly based.

The U.S. Capitol Building's chapel features a stained glass portraying George Washington, while Commander of the Continental Army, kneeling to pray below the phrase: *This Nation Under God.*

In 1864 President Abraham Lincoln said the Bible is "...the best gift God has given to men...but for it we could not know right from wrong."

In the mid 1860's the USA was a nation of predominantly Christian individuals governed by predominantly Christian principles.

Toward the end of the Civil War, Ulysses S. Grant became Commander of the Union Army. He was later elected as the 18th U.S. President. He realized that without faith in the Word of God, America's freedoms would be in grave jeopardy and warned Americans to "Hold fast to the Bible as the sheet anchor of your liberties..."

Due to delays brought about by the *War To Free The Slaves*, the memorial honoring George Washington, the cornerstone of which was laid down during 1848, was not completed until 1884. A great piece of American history is seen in this structure.

Today, visitors can see, about a third of the way up the 545 foot-tall monument, there is a discernable change in the color of the stone. This is because, following the Civil War, a different colored stone was used to complete the structure. This change in shade pinpoints the time when, following the sacrifice of hundreds of thousands of its citizens' lives, the nation lived up to its Founding Fathers Bible-based belief, penned into the Declaration of Independence, that, "All men are created equal and endowed by their creator with certain unalienable rights."

America's school children should be taught these God-honoring and nation-building facts which would bring Americans together, as opposed to the rewritten history which is designed to cause division and push Americans apart from one another.

At the 1884 dedication ceremony an aluminum cap was placed upon the pyramid-shaped top of the Washington Memorial. Engraved into the east-facing side of the cap, 545 feet above Washington, D.C., are the Latin words *Laus Deo*. These words are the first things lit by the rays of the sun every morning in the nation's capital and have been since 1884. *Laus Deo* translates, ***Praise Be To God.***

Inside of the Library of Congress a bronze statue of Moses, holding the Ten Commandments, overlooks the Main Reading Room. The Library's walls are engraved with Bible verses such as: ***The heavens declare the glory of God, and the firmament showeth His handiwork.*** Psalm 19:1, and ***What doth the Lord require of thee, but to do justly, and to love mercy, and to walk humbly with thy God.*** Micah 6:8

Beautiful plaques, designed to bring glory to the Christian God, are seen in the library as well. One proclaims: *One God, One Law, One Element and One Far Off Divine Event To Which The Whole Creation Moves.* Another plaque attests: *Ignorance Is The Curse Of God; Knowledge The Wing Wherewith We Fly To Heaven.*

The Library of Congress's Great Hall in the Thomas Jefferson Building was completed in 1897. The Gutenberg Bible is on permanent display there and several scriptural verses are found etched into its granite walls to include:

Wisdom is the principle thing; therefore, get wisdom and with all thy getting, get understanding. Proverbs 4:7

The light shineth in darkness, and the darkness comprehendeth it not. John 1:5

William McKinley, the 25th U.S. president, confirmed his faith in Psalm 33:12, which reads, ***Blessed is the nation whose God is the LORD...*** when he proclaimed, "The more profoundly we study this wonderful book (the Bible) and the more closely we observe its divine precepts, the better citizens we will become and the higher will be our destiny as a nation."

In the early 1900's, Supreme Court Justice David Brewer stated, "The American nation from its first settlement at Jamestown to this hour is based upon and permeated by the principles of the Bible."

As the twentieth century dawned, the USA was a nation of predominantly Christian men and women governed by predominantly Christian values.

Arlington National Cemetery contains tens of thousands of Christian crosses. The Tomb of the Unknowns, also referred to as the *Tomb for the Unknown Soldiers*, is seen at the Cemetery. Approved by the U.S. Congress in 1921, the words, *Here Rests In Honored Glory An American Soldier Known But To God* are carved into the white marble tomb.

A grateful nation honored the memory of President Abraham Lincoln with a memorial dedicated during 1922. Engraved in the stone wall to Lincoln's right is his famous Gettysburg Address, which ends "...this nation, under God, shall have a new birth of freedom; and that government of the people, by the people, for the people, shall not perish from the earth."

Engraved into the granite wall to President Lincoln's left is his second inaugural address which he delivered in Washington, D.C. on March 4, 1865. Though only 703 words in length, the address contains two complete Bible verses and fourteen references to the Christian God.

It was from the steps of the Lincoln Memorial that Baptist pastor, and Nobel Prize winner, Dr. Martin Luther King, Jr. delivered his powerful *I have a dream* speech. The speech, delivered on August 28, 1963, was based on Isaiah 40:4-5 which reads in part, "I have a dream that one day...the glory of the Lord shall be revealed and all flesh shall see it together."

* In the **End Notes** section you will find the text of President Lincoln's second inaugural address and the text of Dr. King's famous speech.

From 1923 to 1929 Calvin Coolidge served as America's 30th president. President Coolidge stated, "The foundations of our society and our government rest so much on the teachings of the Bible that it would be difficult to support them if faith in these teachings would cease to be practically universal in our country."

President Coolidge said, regarding America's Founding Fathers, "They were intent upon establishing a Christian commonwealth in accordance with the principle of self- government. They were an inspired body of men. It has been said that God sifted the nations that He might send choice grain into the wilderness..."

During 1935, the National Archives Building, where the Declaration of Independence and the U.S. Constitution are stored, was opened. A bronze depiction of the Ten Commandments adorns the entryway floor as these biblical principles served as the foundation for both the U.S. Constitution and the original U.S. legal system.

The building housing the Supreme Court was also dedicated in 1935. Above the eastern entrance, carved in stone, are figures of history's greatest lawmakers. Moses is seated in the center holding a depiction of the Ten Commandments. To enter the courtroom visitors must pass through two large oak doors which have depictions of the Ten Commandments engraved into them. Other engravings, seen directly above the Justices benches, include Moses holding the Ten Commandments.

For 200 years the U.S. Supreme Court has begun each day with a Court Marshal proclaiming, "God save the United States and this honorable court."

Elected as the 32nd U.S. President, Franklin D. Roosevelt, affectionately known as FDR, guided the nation through the Great Depression and most of World War II. He served four terms from 1932 until his death in 1945.

FDR was a man of strong religious faith and he had the fireplace mantle in the White House dining room engraved with a prayer from the nation's second president, John Adams. The prayer reads: *I pray to heaven to bestow the best of blessings on this house and all that hereafter inhabit it.*

During a national radio address on May 27, 1941, he told the nation the Nazis "...are as ruthless as the Communists in the denial of God." He added the coming war would be "... between human slavery and human freedom..." and that America would side with "human freedom, which is the Christian ideal."

Dwight Eisenhower was the Supreme Commander of Allied Forces in Europe during World War II. He ended his speech to the D-Day invasion forces with the exhortation, "...let us all beseech the blessing of Almighty God upon this great and noble undertaking."

Following the D-Day invasion, FDR led America in prayer, seeking God and asking for his fellow Americans, "Almighty God, our sons, pride of our nation, this day have set upon a mighty endeavor, a struggle to preserve our republic, our religion, and...I ask that our people devote themselves in a continuance of prayer."

My personal favorite of the memorials in Washington, D.C. is the Thomas Jefferson Memorial which was dedicated during 1943.

The Jefferson Memorial contains four stone panels that are inscribed with quotes from Jefferson. Three of the quotes refer to God.

1] "We hold these truths to be self-evident: That all men are created equal and are endowed by their Creator with certain unalienable rights." (From the Declaration of Independence of which Jefferson is considered to be the principle author).

2] "Almighty God hath created the mind free...attempts to influence it by temporal punishments...are a departure from the plan of the Holy Author of our religion..." (From a bill on religious freedom).

3] "God who gave us life gave us liberty. Can the liberties of a nation be secure when we have removed a conviction these liberties are the gift of God?" (The answer is a resounding NO)!

A quote from a letter written in 1800 by Jefferson to Founding Father Dr. Benjamin Rush rings the inside of the stone monument. In letters 25 inches tall it reads: "I have sworn upon the altar of God, eternal hostility against every form of tyranny over the minds of man."

In the 1940's the USA was still a nation of predominantly Christian citizens who were governed on predominantly Christian principles.

Harry Truman was the 33rd president of the USA. During 1946, *Give em hell Harry* said, "If men and nations would but live by the precepts of the ancient prophets and the teachings of the Sermon on the Mount, problems which now seem so difficult would soon disappear... The Protestant church, the Catholic church, and the Jewish synagogue...must provide the shock forces to accomplish this moral and spiritual awakening. No other agency can do it. Unless it is done, we are headed for the disaster we would deserve."

During the 1950 Attorney General's Conference, President Truman stated, "The fundamental basis of this nation's law was given to Moses on the Mount...If we don't have the proper fundamental moral background, we will finally end up with a totalitarian government..."

In 1952 Supreme Court Justice William O. Douglas wrote, "We are a religious people and our institutions presuppose a supreme being..."

Delivered during a speech in Abilene, Kansas on June 4, 1952, Dwight D. Eisenhower, who was to soon become the 34th president of the United States, declared, "The real fire within the builders of America was...faith in themselves as children of God..."

In Galations 3:26 we learn:
For ye are all the children of God by faith in Christ Jesus.

President Eisenhower encouraged the U.S. Congress to add the words *under God* to the Pledge of Allegiance, which was recited every day in public schools across the *Home of the Brave*. The primary goal was to make a clear distinction between America's Creator-given freedoms and the atheistic tyrannies of communist regimes that were murdering millions of their own citizens throughout the world.

John F. Kennedy was elected as the 35th U.S. President in 1960. At his inaugural address in January of 1961 President Kennedy said, "The rights of man come not from the generosity of the state but from the hand of God." He concluded: "...let us go forth to lead the land we love, asking His blessing and His help but knowing that here on earth, God's work must truly be our own."

Gerald Ford was the 38th president of the USA. In December of 1974 he quoted the following from a 1955 speech presented by President Eisenhower: "Without God there could be no American form of government, nor an American way of life. Recognition of the Supreme Being is the first, the most basic, expression of Americanism. Thus, the founding fathers of America saw it, and thus with God's help it will continue to be."

As of this writing, coins minted for the USA still proclaim, *In God We Trust.*

I feel it fair to say that a vast amount of historical evidence supports that the United States of America was founded by predominantly Christian men and women on predominantly Christian principles. It is only out of deceit or ignorance that anyone would say otherwise. Yet the deceitful forces opposed to America's God given freedoms are relentless.

Roger Baldwin, founder of the American Civil Liberties Union (ACLU) proclaimed, "Communism is the goal."

This brings us back again to what Karl Marx, the Father of Communism, believed: People without a heritage are easily persuaded and the first battlefield is the rewriting of a nation's history.

Forces unfriendly to the freedoms granted to American citizens knew that people without a heritage could easily be persuaded as they would not realize what they inherited, or what they stood to lose. Such people would not see the worth of defending their way of life. These forces set about gaining influential positions where they could orchestrate the rewriting of America's history.

During 1869, ten years after Darwin's *The Origin Of The Species By Means of Natural Selection: or The Preservation Of Favoured Races In The Struggle For Life* was published, Harvard appointed a new president by the name of Charles Eliot.

The next year Eliot appointed Christopher Columbus Langdell as Dean of Harvard's Law School. Though there were more qualified candidates, Langdell had one common passion with Eliot: both dedicated themselves to making *billions of years leading to Darwinism* the new foundation of both the American educational and legal systems.

Langdell introduced Case Law Study into the American legal system. Until then American Juris Prudence had been based upon the never-changing Ten Commandments. Case Law holds that the law *evolves* case by case and is the reason two people may commit the same crime yet receive widely varying terms of punishment.

Case Law also played a major role in getting prayer and biblical Creation removed from America's public education system.

In 1947 the Supreme Court discovered a supposed *separation of church and state* in the First Amendment of the U.S. Constitution while hearing a case over the use of federal funding to support religious school activities. The ruling was influenced by a personal letter Thomas Jefferson wrote to a pastor he knew during January of 1802. This was a personal letter which was not endorsed by either the House or the Senate.

*In the **End Notes** section you will find the text of President Jefferson's personal letter which was used to erect a wall of separation between church and state.

Though not generally acknowledged today, the court employed this *separation of church and state* to uphold using federal funds to support religious school activities (Everson vs. Board of Education, 330 U.S. 1)!

However, the law soon *evolved* and during 1962 the Supreme Court cited the same *separation of church and state* to outlaw prayer in public schools (Engel v. Vitale 370 U.S. 421). The consequences of this watershed moment cannot be overstated.

The following year, 1963, marked a major *line of demarcation* in the history of the USA as the nation officially turned its back on the God of the Bible who had blessed the country so abundantly.

In a dramatic legal slight-of-hand, prayer to the Creator, who the Founding Fathers declared gave American citizens their Rights, was banned from the nation's public schools. And with prayer went the Creator and the foundations for why we need a redeeming Savior.

Biblical Creation and prayer were then replaced with the philosophical foundation of Humanism which is *billions of years leading to Darwinian evolution* as America began teaching its children there was not a Creator, that man's sin had not brought death into a perfect creation, and that death had actually brought them into existence.

In November of 2006 the *New York Times* quoted Carolyn Porco of the Space Science Institute as saying we must teach, "...our children from a very young age about the story of the universe... more glorious and awesome...than anything offered by any Scripture or god..."

And this is what Humanists have been officially doing through America's Public Education System since 1963. American citizens born since 1945 have been victimized while, as unsuspecting children, they put their faith in their nations' public schools, schools their parents mistakenly trusted.

Beware lest any man spoil you through philosophy and vain deceit, after the tradition of men, after the rudiments of the world, and not after Christ. Colossians 2:8

Some of the fruit growing from the 1963 events include: teenage suicide rates have tripled, teen pregnancies are up 550%, births are up 100% (most are killing their own children), and almost 90% of Christian-raised kids now leave the Church by the age of twenty. (I cover many of the results in my teaching, *The Evil Fruit of Old-Earth Beliefs*).

I received this email from another victim of the false teachings and rewritten history put forth through the USA's public education system: "You make Americans stupid by convincing weak-minded people your invisible god created the world. Face it, Darwinism is a proven fact!"

This is basically what is taught in America's public schools. To help such victims I scientifically destroy the religious philosophies of *billions of years leading to Darwinism* in our DVD teachings, *An Old Earth or A Global Flood* and *Science versus Darwinism in the Textbooks.*

The Humanists responsible for the rewriting of America's past are methodically erasing God's fingerprints from that history. They have deftly employed America's public education system to change the country's collective view from a biblical worldview to a secular view.

For an eye-opening look at what has taken place through our public schools, see my teaching titled, *Public Education Menticide*. The word *menticide* is defined as the deliberate and systematic undermining of a person's beliefs and values.

The forces opposed to America's God given freedoms are relentless. The ACLU shared their first offices in New York with the Communist newspaper *The Masses* during the 1920's. Original ACLU members included Max Eastman, Editor of *The Masses*, and William Foster, Chairman of the Communist Party of America.

Some of the ACLU's prominent legal "victories" include:

- 1963: Prayer and Creation banned from public schools
- 1976: Christmas displays banned from public schools
- 1980: Ten Commandments banned from public schools
- 1986: Religious invocations banned from public schools

While keeping in mind that people without a heritage are easily persuaded, honestly ask yourself, have these rulings helped American society or harmed the nation?

Since 1963, when America failed to stand up for their Creator, here is a look at what has NOT been etched into marble and granite, or inscribed in brass in Washington, D.C.

Dedicated in 1982, the Vietnam Veterans Memorial does not contain a single reference to God.

Dedicated during 1997, the FDR Memorial, though containing a brief reference to the *freedom of worship*, contains no reference to God.

During World War II, from 1941-1945, the U.S. Government issued more than 17 million Bibles to American military personnel around the globe. The World War II Memorial was dedicated in 2004. It does not contain a single reference to God.

Inside the Washington Monument is a plaque which informs visitors about the aluminum cap that was placed atop the monument during its dedication ceremony in 1884. The plague originally read: *The builders searched for an appropriate metal for the apex that would not tarnish and would act as a lightning rod. They chose one of the rarest metals of the time, aluminum. The casting was inscribed with the phrase, Laus Deo (Praise be to God).*

However, during 2008, the wording, *The casting was inscribed with the phrase, Laus Deo (Praise be to God) was* removed from the plaque.

The fool hath said in his heart, There is no God; They are corrupt, they have done abominable works, there is none that doeth good. Psalms 14:1

The fact is the USA is involved in the greatest war of all time, and most Americans do not even realize the battle is raging because this struggle is not a battle of bullets, jet fighters and nuclear bombs. It is much more serious than that. This is the battle between the secular worldview, based upon billions *of years leading to Darwinian-style evolution*, and the biblical worldview, based upon the **COS†** leading to the Gospel of the one and only redeeming Savior, Lord Jesus the Christ.

There have already been billions of victims lost in this war, and they have been lost for eternity. At stake is the soul of every human alive today, as well as the soul of every person to exist in the future.

Since 1963 the foundational philosophies of the secular worldview have been taught as science in America's educational establishments and now dominate, often times through name-calling and blackmail, America's scientific establishment as well.

The secular teachings dominate public institutions and the media (television, newspapers, magazines) and are even in kid's cartoons.

On August 23, 1984, America's 40th President, Ronald Reagan, told Americans, "Without God, democracy will not and cannot long endure. If we ever forget that we're one nation under God, then we will be a nation gone under."

This is a dire situation for America's citizens. I believe if the USA continues down the road it has been on, the nation will lose its God-given rights and the world will lose what has served as God's *city on a hill* for more than 200 years.

The theft of America's heritage is evil fruit being cultivated from the corrupt tree of *death before Adam* beliefs.

In the next Chapter I will discuss what I consider to be the ultimate evil fruit being reaped from the tree of *billions of years leading to Darwinism.*

Chapter Fifteen

The Ultimate Evil Fruit: The Compromise of God's Word In Today's Church

Evolution makes it pretty clear that in nature, and in the moral experience of human beings, there never was any such paradise to be lost.   Dr. John Schneider, former professor at Calvin College who denies Adam and Eve were real people. [96]

Many people were upset by Dr. Schneider's remarks. However, another fruit of *billions of years leading to Darwinism* is that false, secular-based teachings are now engrained in seminaries and Christian colleges which seek to be accepted by A m e r i c a ' s secular society.

And be not conformed to this world: but be ye transformed by the renewing of your mind, that ye may prove what is that good, and acceptable, and perfect, will of God. Romans 12:2

Many of today's church leaders claim that the Creation accounts found in the Book of Genesis, the very foundational pillars that led to Jesus' redeeming sacrifice on the cross, are *nonessential*. It is a dismal state of affairs within the institutionalized Christian Church.

In my opinion, the vilest of the fruit coming from *death before Adam,* old-earth beliefs is the skepticism of God's Word which is now deeply engrained within the organized church.

Sadly, over the past fifty years more and more Christian colleges and seminaries have capitulated with old-earth beliefs that place death before Adam. As a result, up and coming Christian leaders are not taught that mankind's original sin corrupted God's Creation while separating us from our Creator requiring our redemption with Him (the **COS†**). And any awareness of these issues they brought with them to the school is undermined while they attend the institution.

Graduates of compromising establishments have taken on

leadership roles in churches, spreading the false, *death before Adam* teachings like a wildfire.

As atheist Richard Bozarth stated, "Destroy…original sin…If Jesus was not the redeemer who died for our sins, and this is what evolution means, then Christianity is nothing!"

Frank Zindler, Editor of *American Atheist Journal*, and speaker at *The Godless March on Washington* in 1996 stated, "If there never was…an original sin…there is no need of salvation…that puts Jesus…into the ranks of the unemployed."

Both Mr. Bozarth and Mr. Zindler are correct in their observations because, if *billions of years* of death took place prior to mankind's arrival, there was never an original sin which separated us from our Creator requiring our redemption with Him. *Death before Adam* beliefs erode the **COS†** and Scripturally-based Christianity.

If, as a reader, you only take one thing from this writing, I hope that you now understand that, though Darwinism and *billions of years* beliefs are foundational attacks on the authority of the Word of God, the key issue is: ***When did death enter the world, before Adam existed or following his original sin?***

This makes both the *age of the earth* and *Darwinian* issues, while important, somewhat diversionary topics. People debate these subjects while missing the key point which is that placing death before Adam eliminates that it was the first Adam's first sin that allowed death into God's perfect Creation, separating mankind from our Creator, and leading to the need of the second Adam, the Lord Jesus.

For since by man came death, by man came also the resurrection of the dead. For as in Adam all die, even so in Christ shall all be made alive. 1 Corinthians 15:21-22

Death before Adam undermines this Gospel principle. *Billions of years* and Darwinian-style evolution place death prior to the arrival of man. *When* death entered the world is a bottom line issue.

My prayer is that God will use this book to shine the light of Truth onto the compromise positions that are deceiving many people within the Christian community. Only by illuminating the Truth we can evangelize today's organized church.

...teach no other doctrine, Neither give heed to fables and endless genealogies, which minister questions, rather than godly edifying which is in faith... 1 Timothy 3: 3-4

The fact is that time is the glue that holds Atheists, Darwinists, Humanists, Theistic Evolutionists, Progressive Creationists, Naturalists and Gap Theorists together. They each build their faith on long ages of time, accepting that death existed before man.

If I profess with the loudest voice and clearest exposition every portion of the truth of God except precisely that little point which the world and the devil are at that moment attacking, I am not confessing Christ, however boldly I may be professing Christ. Attributed to Martin Luther

Since 1998, I have observed the numbers of Christian-raised kids leaving the church by the age of twenty grow from 71% to about 87%. But even more disturbing is the fact that 98% of churches refuse to allow the life-changing, God-honoring information that God has given me to be shared with their people. Please bear with me while I explain the situation.

For several years I could not understand how a Believer in a leadership position within God's Church could sit back and allow the great majority of the children in their flock to be lost, while blocking the information that would turn most of them around.

To be honest, I used to wrongly think the leaders were simply hirelings or apostates. However, during a trip to the Pacific

Northwest, God revealed the issue to me quite clearly.

While on the road, I shared messages at five churches over five consecutive nights. On three of those evenings the pastor came to me after I spoke and each basically said, **"Russ, I really didn't see any reason to waste time talking about the *Creation-evolution, age of the earth* issues. But you just showed me this is the foundation for everything!"**

I was somewhat dumbfounded that these pastors had not known this. Yet they were sincere, dedicated Believers. I was perplexed as I smiled and said, "Well, I hope what I shared tonight will be a blessing to everyone who was here."

Then, a couple of days later God revealed more of the situation to me. As Jesus asked rhetorically in John 3:12

If I have told you earthly things, and ye believe not, how shall ye believe, if I tell you of heavenly things?

For the past 150 years an ever increasing number of Christian schools and seminaries, not wanting to be called *unscientific, fundamentalist* or some other unflattering name, have opted to compromise Scripture with non-biblical, old-earth beliefs, usually denying God's global judgment by water as well.

Fruit from the various compromised positions includes that many Christian leaders do not understand the **COS†**, the importance of when death entered the Creation, or whether or not there was a global Flood. Such misinformed leaders consider the Book of Genesis to be a non-essential even though *Jesus Christ and every New Testament author refer to Genesis as being historically factual!*

The glaring truth is that both Jesus and all New Testament authors were wrong or the compromised beliefs are wrong. And this book provides the information needed for an open-minded person to make a fact-based decision.

Consider some of the implications of such Christian compromise. Once a Christian school teaches death existed before Adam, as old-earth beliefs do, they cannot logically teach there was an original sin that brought death into the world or separated us from our Creator.

Though old-earth compromisers can still teach Jesus died so our sin could be forgiven, they have no basis for teaching Jesus died on the cross in order to defeat death and redeem us with our Creator.

Even worse, because the compromises are based on man's erroneous interpretations of the earth's strata layers, the students are taught: a) to deny the global Flood, and b) discussing creation, evolution and *age of the earth* issues are divisive and best to be avoided.

Thus the foundations have been destroyed in these Christian institutions. Even worse, the misinformed graduates of such organizations have spread like a deadly cancer throughout churches around the globe. This is why most churches block the information I, and other God-honoring creationists, share.

Jesus lamented in John 5:46-47: ***For had ye believed Moses, ye would have believed me: for he wrote of me. But if ye believe not his writings, how shall ye believe my words?***

Another consequence of compromising God's Word with old-earth beliefs is that sincere, but deceived graduates have been filling church leadership roles. Though they know Jesus died to redeem us with God they do not realize that old-earth beliefs place death before Adam, undermining that Adam's sin allowed death to enter God's Creation while separating us from Him, the reason redemption was needed. The result is they see no reason to discuss such *divisive* issues and block the information.

Then there are the deliberate compromisers of God's Word who become hostile if their non-biblical, old-earth beliefs are challenged. My experience has shown that a single such person can easily create enough conflict to cause church leaders to compromise in order to avoid such a *divisive* issue. All the while the *death before Adam* beliefs continue to flourish.

This is Saul Alinsky's Rules for Radicals at work within the Church.

In a chain reaction effect, another fruit is that while children are having *billions of years leading to Darwinism* pounded into their heads on a daily basis, many church leaders do not see any reason to *waste time* talking about the creation-evolution, *age of the earth* issues. And the great majority of Christian children and grandchildren are lost, many for eternity.

Think about this situation. Teaching that Jesus is the Creator, Judge and redeeming Savior He claims to be is becoming taboo in today's institutionalized church! Thus, the compromise of Scripture within the church is the ultimate fruit of the *billions of years leading to Darwinism* tree.

Thomas Huxley, known as *Darwin's Bulldog* for his aggressive promotion of Darwinism and his contempt for Christianity, commented on the church's attempts to compromise with old-earth beliefs. He said, "The position they have taken up is hopelessly untenable."

Then, reading from 1 Corinthians 15:21-22, he noted: **For since by man came death, by man came also the resurrection of the dead. For as in Adam all die, even so in Christ shall all be made alive.**

Huxley then rhetorically asked, "If Adam may be held to be no more real a personage than Prometheus... what value has Paul's dialectic?"[98]

The obvious answer is there is no value in the biblical message if *billions of years* of death existed prior to man's original sin. Still, many Christian institutions are teaching old-earth beliefs that place death before Adam.

A professor at a well-known Christian university that teaches old-earth beliefs wrote the following message to a pastor who had hosted me. The professor's statements are in bold type; my responses are italicized.

The young earth *(Bible believing)* **creationist you hosted stated death prior to Adam would pose a problem for Christian theology.** *Old-earth beliefs place death and evil before Adam. This negates the Gospel's foundations that God created a perfect universe with no death or evil in it, reflecting His perfect nature. Then Adam's sin corrupted the Creation, separating us from God while allowing death and evil to enter. Because of God's grace, He sent Jesus to receive our punishment and defeat death so those who accept Him as Lord will be redeemed with Him for eternity.* **Doesn't eating plants kill them?** *Plants were designed as food (Gen 1:30). Man has a living soul, a term not used for plants.*

Gen 2:17"...in the day you eat of it, you shall surely die..." doesn't refer to physical death (Adam did not physically die until hundreds of years later) but SPIRITUAL death. *God was referring to both. Spiritual death was the immediate wage of sin. Physical death was the merciful callback to our loving Creator so we do not live in sin, separated from God, forever. As a branch cut from the vine wilts away over time, physical death allows us time to accept redemption with God through our redeeming Savior.* **Romans 5:12 only refers to man's death.** *While the Bible is referring specifically to man's death, nowhere in Scripture is there any hint of animal death before Adam's original sin which brought death and decay to "the whole creation" (Gen 3:17-20; Rom 8:20-22).*

The complete absence of physical death could only occur in a world quite unlike the one we live in. *ABSOLUTELY! The original Creation was much different from the fallen, cursed, post-Flood world we endure today. Jesus will soon give us an earth where there shall be no more death (Rev 21) and where the lion shall eat straw (plants) like an ox (Isaiah 11).* **Face it, there was evil in the world prior to Adam's fall through Lucifer's rebellion in heaven.** *Scripture tells us God considered His Creation very good at the end of the sixth day. It was NOT full of*

Satan and his minions, evil and death. (I will discuss the misguided Gap Theory later in this chapter).

I suggest we not waste our time on *age of the earth* **issues.** *With 87% of Christian kids leaving the church by age 20, with 95% of churchgoers and 60% of pastors holding a secular worldview, and with old-earth beliefs serving as the foundation for this skepticism, as for me and my house, we will continue to serve our Creator, Judge and redeeming Savior, whose Word begins by declaring, "In the beginning God created..."*

The lack of biblical knowledge expressed by this Christian college professor is a direct fruit of compromising with old-earth beliefs and is held by most of the graduates of these institutions.

Not wanting to *"waste time"* discussing parts of the Bible that they do not believe, they cause the information I share to be blocked while accepting the loss of almost 90% of Christian children.

And why are our kids deserting the Church?

Enlightening statistics are supplied in *The Bridger Generation: America's Second Largest Generation, What They Believe, How to Reach Them* by Thom Rainer. Of American citizens born from **1927 to 1945 – 65% attend a Christian church.** These people graduated high school before the removal of Biblical Creation and before the indoctrination in *billions of years* and Darwinian evolution officially began.

1946 to 1964 – 35% attend a Christian church. These citizens were partway through the public education system when the official indoctrination in the secular worldview began. Most of their teachers had been educated with a biblical worldview.

1965 to 1983 – 16% attend a Christian church. This was the first group of American children fully indoctrinated by *billions of years* leading to Darwinian evolutionism.

1984 to 2002 – 4% attend a Christian church. These victims were fully indoctrinated in secular teachings by teachers who were also educated in *billions of years leading to Darwinism.*

Teaching children it is a scientific fact that death brought mankind into existence has consequences.

In 2 Timothy 4:3-4 we are told: ***For the time will come when they will not endure sound doctrine; but after their own lusts shall they heap to themselves teachers, having itching ears; And they shall turn away their ears from the truth, and shall be turned unto fables.***

Fitting these verses from 2 Timothy to a tee, a pastor sent me this note: "Because of the diversity of theology and scriptural understanding of our members we accept creation may have occurred over a long period of time and are not interested in your messages."

I think the *diversity of theology and scriptural understanding* within this congregation is actually the reason why they should invite me t o share on a Sunday morning. Instead, the well-meaning attendees are not allowed to see that God's Word trumps secular teachings and are, instead, allowed to believe whatever they like, and are led to think doing so is perfectly acceptable to God.

Barna Research conducted a nationwide poll of conservative-oriented churches during 2006. The results revealed the growing skepticism within today's Church. A series of questions were asked such as:

Do you believe that: Scripture is the inerrant Word of God; God is omnipotent and omniscient; absolute moral truth exists; Jesus lived a sinless life?

If a person responded *yes* to these questions that person was considered to hold a biblical worldview. If a person responded *no* to any question, he or she was considered as not holding a biblical worldview.

The results revealed that 49% of pastors, 67% of seminary graduates, 95% of Christian adults and 96% of born-again teenagers do not hold a biblical worldview. [97]

160

Secularism is alive and well in Christian homes, churches, schools and seminaries.

The statistics reveal that some of the fruit being reaped from the false science which has been sewn through America's public educational system since 1963 includes that even the faith of many Christians has been eroded in the pillars of Christianity, the **COSt**.

The Gap Theory, Theistic Evolution, and Progressive Creation are some of the ultimate fruit from the old-earth tree and are deeply engrained throughout today's Church.

A generous individual offered to donate one of our God-honoring luxury bus trips to Grand Canyon to a Christian seminary that teaches old-earth beliefs.

On these tours I cover the global Flood, how Grand Canyon formed quickly, the missing mile of strata, the Grand Staircase (see Chapter 4) and much more. In all, the day leaves guests with the Truth of God's uncompromised Word. The donor was hopeful they would see the Truth of Scripture through the information I share during the trip. Fifty-five of their students or faculty could have gone on the one-day tour for free.

The seminary said, "No, thanks."

Once a Christian college or seminary teaches students death existed before Adam, as old-earth beliefs imply, they cannot logically teach God's perfect (**C**)reation was corrupted by Adam's (**O**)riginal Sin which (**S**)eparated us from God (while allowing death to enter the world) requiring that we be † (the Cross of Christ) redeemed with our loving Creator, Lord Jesus the Christ.

To try and get around the roadblock created by their compromise with *death before Adam* beliefs, two professors at Calvin College, which promotes Theistic Evolutionism, announced they do not believe there was an Adam or Eve, stating, "We know because evolution has taught us."[99]

Be mindful that in Mark 13:22, when the disciples asked Jesus for the signs of the end times, just before His return, Jesus warned: ***For false Christs and false prophets shall rise, and shall shew signs and wonders, to seduce, if it were possible, even the elect.***

Anti-Christ doesn't mean *against Christ*, it means *instead of Christ*. Jesus warned false Christs would mislead people in the last days and any Jesus other than the one presented in the Bible is a likely candidate to be an *anti-Christ*.

As a recovered Theistic Evolutionist, my advice is, *put your faith in the uncompromised Word of God, word for word and cover to cover.*

Since a convincing lie contains 95% truth, I would expect a false Christ to be 95% the same as the biblical Jesus. Thus, we must be as the Bereans in Acts 17:10-11, who thoughtfully ***received the word with all readiness of mind, and searched the scriptures daily, whether those things were so.***

We must compare the things we see and hear to God's Word to ensure that what we believe is in line with the Word of our Creator and Savior.

In doing so, from Genesis we know the only Jesus found in Scripture created the heavens and earth in six days and judged man's sin with a Flood; whereby, all the high hills, that were under the whole heaven, were covered.

To help those who are struggling with the Gap Theory, Theistic Evolution, Progressive Creation **or any other non-biblical belief** *(I say this as a wake-up call, not as an insult),* following are some things to consider about these man-made creators.

Progressive Creationism is the belief that the Creator of the world used *billions of years* of death and suffering to gradually create everything, ending with mankind. There are varying versions, but in general they either believe each day of Creation was a long era of time (Day Age theories) or that there were long periods of time between each literal Creation day.

Progressive Creationism does not fit the evidence or Scripture, undermines people's faith in the **COSt**, and opposes the words of the Lord Jesus who claimed man was made in the beginning (Mark 10:6).

Theistic Evolutionism is the belief that the Creator of the world used *billions of years* of death and suffering to gradually evolve everything, ending with mankind. Theistic Evolutionists have no more proof of macro-evolution having occurred than do atheistic Darwinists. This belief is non-Scriptural, undermines people's faith in the **COSt**, and is opposed to the words of the Lord Jesus who claimed man was made since the beginning (Matthew 19:4).

The Gap Theory claims there was a creation before the Creation found in God's Word. Millions of Hebrew experts, who lived before Secularists began claiming the earth's strata formed over *billions of years* of time, did not find this supposed Gap. All the same, Gap Theorists believe Satan was cast down to the non-biblical creation where Satan and his minions so corrupted the world that God destroyed it and started over with a second Creation.

This is where the Gap theory picks up with God's actual Word. They claim God made a second Creation (the only one mentioned in the Scriptures) starting in Genesis 1:2 which He completed in six days, deeming it *very good*, yet leaving it full of Satan and his minions! Common sense alone destroys the Gap Theory.

The Gap Theory, Progressive Creation, and Theistic Evolution are simply manmade attempts to bend God's Word to fit with secular interpretations of biology and geology (the earth's strata layers). These manmade philosophies undermine people's faith in the pillars of true Christian faith.

The various compromise beliefs also deny the global Flood, or the evidence of the event, as foretold in 2 Peter 3:3-6. The denial is due to the fact that such a Flood destroys this non-biblical, death *before Adam* beliefs.

Let us heed Colossians 2:8 and **beware of man's philosophies which are after the world and not after Christ**.

As Elijah challenged the Jews in 1 Kings 18:21:

How long shalt ye between two opinions? if the LORD be God, follow him: but if Baal, then follow him. And the people answered him not a word.

Atheists, Darwinists, Humanists, Theistic Evolutionists, Progressive Creationists, and Gap Theorists put their faith in *billions of years* of time. It is the glue that binds these beliefs together. But time should be employed to support its Creator, not to undermine people's faith in the Bible.

Casting down imaginations, and every high thing that exalteth itself against the knowledge of God, and bringing into captivity every thought to the obedience of Christ. 2 Corinthians 10:5

By increasing awareness of the Scriptural compromises taking place and by revealing how the global Flood washes away *death before Adam* beliefs, my hope is that God will use this writing as a tool to lead readers to place their total trust in the complete authority of His Word, word for word and cover to cover.

So then faith cometh by hearing, and hearing by the word of God. Romans 10:17

"I'm a retired Pastor and I always taught Theistic Evolution. I truly believed that was how God created us and you just showed me I was completely wrong. Thank you."

Larry in AZ

"We were Theistic Evolutionists for 25 years. After seeing your first 3 seminars, we now know that God created us!"

Bob and Carol in CO

Section III:
Ten Reasons to Believe God's Word: Creation Compared to Science and the Secular Worldview

Introduction to Chapters 16 – 20

In this age of scientific revelation can we truly believe the Biblical foundations, which I refer to as the **COSt**? These are laid down in Genesis 1 and 3, that God's perfect (**C**)reation was corrupted by Adam's (**O**)riginal Sin which (**S**)eparated mankind from God (while allowing death to enter the world) requiring we be **†** (the Cross) redeemed with our loving Creator who is also our redeeming Savior, Lord Jesus the Christ. Can we really believe Jesus is the Creator and Judge the Bible says He is?

Though all Christians believe Jesus died so their sins can be forgiven, many need convincing before they will place their faith in His entire Word.

I have already discussed the global Flood judgment, so allow me to discuss biblical Creation. This affects us more than most people realize. Take the calendars that we live our lives by as an example:

- A day is defined by the earth's spin on its axis.
- A month is roughly defined by the moon's revolution a r o u n d the earth.
- A year is defined by the earth's revolution around the sun.

So where does the seven day week come from?

- A week comes from the six days of Creation plus the seventh day of Sabbath rest.

God, as clearly as could be put down in writing, describes His seven days of Creation in the Bible.

Every writer of the New Testament refers to the book of Genesis. Genesis is referred to more than 200 times by these authors. Jesus Christ Himself references Genesis twenty-five times, including how man was made since the beginning.

I do not like to use the term *young earth*. I think an earth six to ten thousand years old is actually quite ancient. After all, only over the past hundred years have people been able to begin enjoying cars, airplanes, radios, television, penicillin, indoor bathrooms and so many more of the things we take for granted today. Just twenty years ago, I did not have a cell phone or personal computer. A world several thousand years old is ancient.

However, in the secular world, people have been indoctrinated to think in terms of *billions of years* of time, time that is truly beyond comprehension.

To be honest, I wanted to write a section titled *The Top Ten Evidences of The Young-Earth Biblical Creation*. However, since I have already covered several great evidences of our young earth such as Grand Canyon, the Grand Staircase, the Ice Age, Dinosaurs and Carbon Dating, it would have been too redundant.

This section will add to and reinforce the simple fact that we can put our trust and faith in the entire Word of God, the Word who became flesh and dwelt among us, our Creator, Judge and redeeming Savior, Lord Jesus the Christ: word for word and cover to cover.

Chapter Sixteen

The Heavens Declare the Glory of God: Our Solar System and the Stars

Our Creator, Judge and Savior is too big to be contained by nature or anything else. Still, His fingerprints are seen throughout His Creation.

Russ Miller

On the fourth day of the Creation week **God made two great lights; the greater light to rule the day, and the lesser light to rule the night...** Genesis 1:16a

The sun is certainly a great light. In fact, 960,000 earths would fit into it. Thankfully, God placed the sun 93 million miles away from the earth.

Though secular astronomy is based on *billions of years* thinking, the actual evidence does not compel anyone to interpret the universe through the secular worldview.

Astrophysicist and geophysicist Dr. John Eddy honestly stated, "I suspect that the sun is 4.5 billion years old...however ...we could live with...(~6,000 years). I don't think that we have much in the way of observational evidence in astronomy to conflict with that."

Take for example the *lesser light to rule the night*, our moon. According to *New Scientist*, signs of volcanic activity indicate that the moon formed *just a few million years ago*.[100] However, signs of volcanic activity could also mean the moon formed just a few thousand years ago.

Evidence that our moon is only a few thousand years old includes short-life lunar isotopes. I previously discussed the radiometric dating methods and how they are based upon the decay rates of radioactive elements. Thorium 230, based on today's observed rate of decay, should turn into lead in about 50,000 years. However, thorium 230 and other short life radioactive elements have been found in rock samples brought back from the moon.

These short-life lunar isotopes are great supporting evidence for the Bible's version of God's Creation. [101] Lunar recession also supports a youthful solar system.

The earth is losing its moon. This is not something you need to be overly concerned about as it is only moving away from earth at a rate of between 4 and 12 inches annually. This means that in the days of Adam and Eve the moon may have been a couple of miles closer to us than it is today.

Lunar recession is a problem for old-earth beliefs. At the current pace of recession, the moon would have been so close to earth 75 million years ago, during the supposed time of the dinosaurs, that the gravitational forces of the moon would have caused ocean tide waters to flood the earth twice per day.

Another problem lunar recession causes for old-earth beliefs concerns the Roche Limit. This principle holds that if the moon were within 11,500 miles of the earth, the tidal friction would cause the moon to shatter. In other words our earth and moon cannot be *billions of years* old.

In Genesis 1:16b we learn that on the fourth day of Creation God

...made the stars also.

The term *star* in this verse could refer to any celestial orb, from what we refer to as stars today to comets, nebulae or planets.

Let's look at some evidence from the planet Jupiter that lends support for Scripturally-based Creation.

Jupiter is about 1,000 times the size of earth and is rapidly cooling down. Research shows that Jupiter is losing heat about twice as fast as it receives warmth from the sun. Yet despite the continual loss of heat, Jupiter has not had the time to become a cold or frozen ball. This is solid proof in favor of biblical Creation, as Jupiter cannot be *billions of years* old.

Jupiter has a moon we refer to as Ganymede that still has a strong magnetic field coming from within it. Though there is debate over the cause, many scientists claim magnetic fields are generated by the motion of molten metal inside an orb. This supports a young solar system, for if the solar system were *billions of years* old, Ganymede should have lost its magnetic field long ago.[102]

Comets also provide supporting proof of biblical Creation. Short-life comets are hurtling through our solar system, and as they travel they are losing material. At the rate at which they are losing matter, they should not exist after more than 10,000 years. However, we still have them today.

The secular view is that the solar system is *billions of years* old. This does not fit with many observable evidences.

To explain why some planets are still hot despite losing massive quantities of heat, the claim has been made that the planets are shrinking, which causes gravitational energy to change into internal heat and radiation. [103]

However, shrinkage cannot produce enough energy to explain why the planets have not cooled down yet. Others have suggested that that helium hitting the core of the planet is releasing energy, or perhaps there is some sort of nuclear fusion taking place. [104] So far a viable *billions of years* interpretation has not been found.

To explain away short life comets, old-universe astronomers invoke that the Ort Cloud is continually producing new comets that either enter our solar system directly or lie in the Kuiper Belt just outside the orbit of Pluto. From there, the comets supposedly supply new comets to our solar system. However, the Ort Cloud has never been observed and goes against mathematical probability.

The Ort Cloud is a non-scientific excuse for why we observe young comets in a solar system which Secularists claim is *billions of years* old.

A Super Nova is an exploded star. Several hundred remnants of exploded stars are observable. At the rate at which star deaths have been observed, the few we see should have taken about 7,000 years to accumulate. The lack of Super Novas is more proof in favor of a young universe. 105

The secular view is that a Big Bang, discussed in Chapter 1, began the universe somewhere between 6 billion and 20 billion years ago. However, if the Big Bang theory were true, the matter in space would be evenly distributed by now. But it is not evenly spread out; instead, the universe is tightly wound up.

Stars throughout the visible universe are seen to be in clusters or in tightly wound spirals, with great empty voids of space between the groups of stars. 106 This is called the Winding Up Dilemma.

In the Milky Way Galaxy, the inner stars are rotating around the center of the galaxy faster than the outer stars. In fact, the rotation speeds are so fast that the Milky Way would have lost its spiral shape and become a featureless disc of stars in less than half a billion years. Secularists teach it is at least 10 billion years old, so this is a dilemma for them. 107

The Winding Up Dilemma supports that the universe is relatively young as the stars have not had time to spread out evenly. This is exactly what would be expected if biblical Creation were true.

We need an understanding of humongous numbers in order to discuss the vastness of God's Creation because as we are told in Isaiah 51:13 (and many other verses as well),

...the LORD thy maker, that hath stretched forth the heavens...

And God did indeed stretch them forth! Our present measuring device for God's universe is the light year. The present speed of light is 186,282 miles per second, and it takes sunlight 8 minutes to travel the 93 million miles to earth. At light's present speed, it will travel 6 trillion miles in one light year.

Six trillion?! I think we can comprehend a million. However, since a *billion* of anything begins to become a bit murky, and we

170

really do not grasp what a trillion of something is, here are some comparisons which helped me get a handle on these huge numbers. Hopefully, these will help you too.

- 1 million seconds ago was about 11 days ago
- 1 billion seconds ago was about 32 years ago
- 1 trillion seconds represents about 32,000 years of time

Yes, there is a vast difference between these numbers. And if the six-trillion miles light travels in a year were represented by seconds, a light year would equal 192,000 years of time. Wow!

And God made...the stars also. Genesis 1:16

Besides our sun, Pollux is one of the closest stars to the earth. It is a mere 34 light years away. This is a nice distance since its diameter is 9 times that of our sun.

Arcturus is a star which God has hurtling 400,000 miles per hour through our Milky Way Galaxy. It is 37 light years away from earth.

God placed Betelgeuse 427 light years away from us. The diameter of this huge star is twice the diameter of the earth's orbit around the sun! It is so large that 262 trillion earths would fit inside of it.

The largest star known to man is VY Canis Majoris. It is so big that it would take light 8 hours to circle it. An estimated seven quadrillion earths would fit into it. But we have not discussed what a quadrillion is, have we?

Using seconds again as our example, a quadrillion seconds would represent 32 million years of time. Thank the Lord He stretched VY Canis Majoris out 5,000 light years away from earth.

The scientific fact is that the heavens are stretched out beyond human understanding, just as the omnipotence of the Creator of those heavens is also beyond our comprehension.

The Hubble Space Telescope floats in space about 353 miles above our planet. Since NASA first aimed the powerful Hubble lens toward the deepest regions of outer space, its pictures have contributed support for Scripturally-based Creation.

After the telescope was aimed at just a tiny fraction of outer space with its lens left open for a 96-hour exposure, the resulting visual was astounding. The picture revealed thousands of tightly wound, mature spiral galaxies, exactly what would be expected had God recently made the heavens mature at His spoken word.

And each individual galaxy is made of billions of individual stars, and each star is billions of miles away from any other star. Again fitting the biblical view of our Creator Who *stretched forth the heavens*, and in Genesis 22, compared the number of stars in heaven to the number of grains of sand on the sea shore:

17 ...I will multiply thy seed as the stars of the heaven, and as the sand which is upon the sea shore...

This verse was given to mankind at a time when only about 1,500 stars could be observed with the naked eye.

We learn from 1 Corinthians 15 that each star is different from every other star:

41 There is one glory of the sun, and another glory of the moon, and another glory of the stars: for one star differeth from another star in glory.

And modern science finds that stars vary by size, heat output, color and other factors which cause each individual star to be unique and different from all other stars. The heavens do indeed reveal the glory of God

The secular view, based on the faulty belief in *billions of years* of time, predicted the pictures coming from the Hubble would reveal the light of the infant universe shortly after the Big Bang.

But rather than saving the Big Bang theory, the pictures crushed the hopeful predictions of Big Bang enthusiasts and old-universe beliefs. The truth is that the heavens declare that our Creator and biblical Savior is too big to be contained by nature.

God's fingerprints can be seen throughout His Creation. We just need to look at things through a biblical worldview by placing our faith in the knowledge and wisdom of God rather than in the limited knowledge and biased wisdom of fallible man.

Is not God in the height of heaven?! and
behold the height of the stars, how high they are.
Job 22:12

Chapter Seventeen

He Formed It To Be Inhabited: The Anthropic Principle, Intelligent Biblical Design, and Kinds

For thus saith the LORD that created the heavens; God himself that formed the earth and made it; he hath established it, he created it not in vain, he formed it to be inhabited...

Isaiah 45:18

Did you know that observable facts support this verse?

The Anthropic Principle holds that the universe appears to have been designed with very specific physical laws and properties which allow life to exist on earth. More specifically, this term comes from the Greek word *anthropos* which means man. Thus, the Anthropic Principle is that the universe appears to have been designed for the existence of mankind.

From the hundreds of examples that could be shown, let me provide a few from our solar system and earth's location in it. Both are just right for life to exist on our planet.

The earth is located within a narrow range of distance from the sun to allow for life to exist here. Of the vast range of temperatures which vary by millions of degrees throughout the universe, from the inside of a star to the depths of outer space, water is only liquid in a narrow 180 degree range.

If earth were too close to the sun, all of our planet's water would evaporate and there would be no life on earth. If we were too far from the sun, all the water on earth would freeze, again preventing life from thriving.

The sun is a unique star that is perfect for the existence of life on earth. Most stars pulsate violently while emitting massive doses of harmful gamma rays, ultraviolet rays, x-rays and other cosmic rays that would end life on any nearby orb. However, the sun is a very evenly operating star which allows for life to thrive on our planet.

Our sun is also just the right size to allow for plants to live on earth. If it were too much smaller, the UV radiation emitted would not be enough to allow for the process of photosynthesis to take place. If the sun were much larger, the radiation it would emit would destroy life on earth.

Our moon is located within a narrow range of distance from the earth to accommodate life on our planet. Earth's tides are caused by the moon's gravity. If the moon were too close, the tides would drown the world twice per day. If the moon were too far away, the tides would weaken to the point they would not help cleanse the oceans. The resulting marine-life disaster would impact all life as the oxygen in the air we breathe is largely replenished by marine plants.

Earth's gravity is perfect for the existence of life on our orb. Our planet is spinning about 1,000 miles per hour at the equator while we hurtle at more than 66,000 miles per hour around the sun (about 30 times as fast as a speeding bullet)! Yet our planet's gravity holds us in place without crushing us, allowing life to continue on earth.

From the larger gas planets in our solar system that protect the earth from stray meteors to the proton-to-neutron balance throughout the universe, hundreds of great evidences could be provided in support of the Anthropic Principle.

The secular view is that there are an infinite number of universes, so despite the mathematical improbability of life existing on our planet, life on earth is not special to the cosmos. However, despite constant claims of inhabitable planets having been detected in the far reaches of space, no such claims have survived the slightest bit of honest scientific scrutiny. The observable evidence is that our solar system was uniquely designed with very specific physical laws and properties which allow life to exist on earth.

Intelligent Biblical Design (IBD)

The Anthropic Principle is solid support for biblical Creation and for our intelligent biblical Designer. While even a wooden chair requires a furniture maker to have designed it, even more so do the intricacies of life demand there was an extremely intelligent designer behind them.

While there is a non-Christian Intelligent Design (ID) movement, of which many Christians are involved, I belong to the Intelligent Biblical Design (IBD) movement.

IBD, like ID, is based on the observable design of things as being the result of an intelligent source rather than the product of naturally occurring processes.

The difference between ID and IBD is that IBD gives the credit to its proper source, Jesus Christ, who made all things as we are told in John 1:3:

All things were made by him; and without him was not any thing made that was made.

Examples of IBD

Let's look at some examples of IBD that I use in my presentation, *Science Compared to God's Word.* You can also find these and other examples of IBD included in our book, *The Darwinian Delusion.* In Genesis 1, we learn that God made plants on the third day of the Creation week:

11 ***And God said, Let the earth bring forth grass, the herb yielding seed, and the fruit tree yielding fruit...***

God then made flying creatures (birds, mammals, reptiles and insects) on the fifth and sixth days of His Creation... ***and fowl that may fly above the earth in the open firmament of heaven.***
Genesis 1:20

Let's consider the Bucket Orchid. This plant has a very slimy surface. When a bee lands on the orchid's petal, the tiny creature slips and falls into in a pool of liquid in the bottom of the flower. The only way for the bee to get out of the liquid and escape from the flower is to crawl up a step found at the edge of the pool that leads into a tunnel. The tunnel is the only route of escape from the orchid's bucket to the outside.

However, as the bee is crawling through the tunnel, the walls contract and hold it prisoner while the flower glues a pair of pollen sacs to the creature's back. After allowing time for the adhesive to dry, the plant releases the bee which continues on through the tunnel and flies away.

If the creature lands on another Bucket Orchid, the entire process takes place again with one small difference. The second time the poor little bee has slipped and fallen into the pool, climbed up the step and crawled into the tunnel only to have the walls capture it again, a hook comes from the flower and removes the pollen sacs to complete the pollination process! 108

That's what I refer to as Intelligent Biblical Design! Psalm 139 praises our intelligent biblical Designer:

14 *I will praise thee; for I am fearfully and wonderfully made*

God made mankind, in His image, on the sixth day of Creation and the wonderful IBD of the human body certainly does glorify our intelligent biblical Designer!

Our brain is a living computer far more complex than anything ever put together by the human intelligence it contains. Yet the human brain is so compactly designed that it only weighs about three pounds.

From the beat of our heart to the twitch of an eye, our brain controls every action. It distinguishes the things that touch our skin, it smells odors in our noses, it receives light waves that enter our eyes and the sounds that are received by our ears and turns all of this into information we can use. Our brain then sends the information, billions of pieces of electronic data, to billions of nerves throughout our body via the central nervous system.

Just as the design seen in a wooden chair is credited to the furniture maker, the wonderful design found in the human body should be used to glorify our intelligent biblical Designer.

The secular view is that complex designs found in all the life forms seen around the world are the result of naturally occurring processes combined with long ages of time (there can never be too much time for Darwinists).

Since life is far too complex to have come about on its own, as I covered in Chapter Seven, let me use a big chunk of rock for a simple explanation of how design demands that there be an intelligent source behind the design.

Mount Rushmore, located in South Dakota, was sculpted out of a granite hillside by Gutzon and Lincoln Borglum between 1927 and 1941. Today, we can enjoy the 60-foot tall busts of former U.S. presidents George Washington, Thomas Jefferson, Abraham Lincoln and Theodore Roosevelt at the park.

If you were standing on one of the viewing platforms at the park and a park ranger were to tell you that the figures were the result of millions of years of rain and wind erosion, you would most likely think the ranger was loony. Why?

Because design of such magnitude could not have occurred by random, natural processes. Even well-designed rock demands that there was a designer behind the design. And life forms are trillions of times more complex than carved stone.

Keep this example in mind the next time a Darwinist tries to convince you that you evolved from a wet rock.

Many Darwinists argue that the ordered structure found in either a tornado, rock crystal or snowflake is proof that complexity and order can occur without God.

However, the observable facts reveal that the order found in non-living systems, such as in a tornado, rock crystal or snowflake, has nothing to do with the order and complexity found in a living system.

Think about it. Tornadoes, rock crystals and snowflakes form naturally, but the order they exhibit is the result of the arrangement of their properties. Living cells, however, form due to the specified complex genetic information contained in their DNA.

Furthermore, unlike life forms, tornadoes, rock crystals and snowflakes do not ingest nutrients to turn into energy, communicate with each other, or breed to produce offspring. Only living things have the ability to digest food and use the nutrients to maintain bodily systems and produce both energy and the genetic data to bring forth offspring after their kind. 109

Observable scientific facts reveal that naturally occurring order does not show that the order and complexity found in the genetic code of a living organism could have developed without our intelligent biblical Designer.

Kinds will bring forth after their kind

And God created every living creature after their kind, and every winged fowl after his kind. Genesis 1:21

Though not a science book, ten times in the book of Genesis we are told that plants or animals will *bring forth after their kind*. If the Bible is the Word of God, biology should find that plants and animals will only reproduce their own kind with variations occurring within their kind. If the observable evidences did not support that *kinds will bring forth after their kind*, Scripture would have been scientifically refuted.

A biblical *kind* is a group of organisms which have been brought forth (descended) from the genetic data God created in the original ancestor. Keep in mind that the term *kind* is a biblical term. Speaking in the language of modern science, a *kind* is closest to a *family*.

So what does the evidence reveal? Today, after millions of scientific observations, all that is found is kinds will only bring forth after their kind. This is reliable, empirical criteria supporting the truth of the Bible.

Any particular kind of plant or animal can bring forth variations within its kind due to the sorting (recombination) or loss (Gene Depletion - see Chapter 9) of the original genetic data. In scientific jargon, *kinds bringing forth after their kind* is referred to as micro-adaptations, micro-evolution (NOT Darwinian-style macro-evolution), horizontal evolution, or variations.

Though variations within a kind can provide a wide range of appearances, one kind only has the genetic information in its DNA to bring forth after its kind. That is, dogs will only produce dogs; cats will only produce cats; pine trees will only produce pine trees, etc.

As an example, you could take a male and female dog (mutts work the best due to their wide gene pool) and selectively breed dogs for 20 years. By breeding the offspring together that have similar features to one another, you would likely have several dozen very different looking dogs at the end of the 20-year period, but they would still be dogs. The differences are representative of micro-changes within the dogs which resulted from the sorting or the loss (Gene Depletion) of the genetic information contained within the gene pools of the two mutts you started with.

The secular view, known as Neo-Darwinism, is that random mutations add massive amounts of new and beneficial genetic information to an organism's gene pool. Then, Natural Selection causes the improved mutant to take over the population, leading to Darwinian style macro-evolution. Though this belief is taught as science in secular schools, no viable examples have ever been found of one kind of organism changing into a different kind of organism (I covered Neo-Darwinism in Chapter Nine).

Meanwhile, a person could show millions of observable examples of scripturally correct micro-adaptations. This makes micro-adaptations a scientific fact as we should expect since ten times in Genesis we are told that plants or animals will bring forth after their kind. 110

"The Sunday I heard you at my church was one of the most important hours of my life. You answered so many questions that I had and you made things so easy to understand. God bless you."

Wes in OR

My twelve year old son was playing outside with his buddies when I called them all in to watch your DVD on 'Science verses Darwinism." At first they groaned about having to watch a lecture but as it played they became riveted, wide-eyed and amazed! They've been talking about it for days."

Tony in FL

Chapter Eighteen

The Earth Was Divided in the Days of Peleg: Division and History

And unto Eber were born two sons: the name of one was Peleg; for in his days was the earth divided... Genesis 10:25

The Earth Was Divided

You may be envisioning the land mass splitting apart, and the global Flood certainly led to a wide separation among the land masses. Oceans, mountains ranges and massive post-Flood volcanic activity carved up the earth's crust like an unfinished jigsaw puzzle.

However, the earth was truly divided in the days of Peleg whose name can mean either *furrowed* or *divided*. It was during Peleg's roughly 239-year lifespan that the people of the world were separated by languages, nations and geographical locations.

In Genesis 8, God told Noah, his family, and the creatures that had been aboard the ark to spread around the world.

16-17 *Go forth of the ark, thou, and thy wife, and thy sons, and thy sons' wives with thee. Bring forth with thee every living thing that is with thee...that they may breed abundantly in the earth, and be fruitful, and multiply upon the earth.*

However, in Genesis 11 we learn that the people rebelled and gathered at one location, Babel. Because of this, God confused their languages at the Tower of Babel. This resulted in the people scattering around the globe.

9 *Therefore is the name of it called Babel; because the LORD did there confound the language of all the earth: and from thence did the LORD scatter them abroad upon the face of all the earth.*

This occurred after the Flood while the earth was still in its Ice Age. I discussed the Ice Age in Chapter 6, so I will only recap a couple of the key points here. Despite the appearance of a frigid Ice Age, most of the earth actually enjoyed a tropical climate during that timeframe. The hot thermal waters from the fountains of the deep had led to very warm oceans and massive evaporation. This resulted in cloud cover which provided rain in the central regions and snow upon the polar areas.

Because of the volume of water located in the Polar Regions in the form of ice and snow, the seas were about 395 feet lower than they are today. Even secular textbooks attest to this. Here is an example, from a secular textbook, I use in my presentation, *An Old Earth or A Global Flood.*

"Twenty thousand years ago...sea level was 120m (395 feet) lower than it is today...ice masses melted and sea level rose..."[111]

Because of the lower seas, much more of the earth's continental shelves were exposed above sea level immediately following the Flood than we find exposed today. This enabled the animals that had been on the ark, and their offspring, to quickly spread around the planet. After the confusion of languages at the Tower of Babel, the lower oceans allowed people to scatter around the earth as well.

As the world's oceans cooled down, the evaporation slowed, and the Ice Age came to an end about 400 to 600 years after the Flood ended. As the ice caps began melting, the water filled the seas, and the earth was divided by languages, nations, islands and continents.

An important question I am often asked is, if we are all descended from Adam and Eve, where did the different races come from?

Let me be perfectly clear. We did not evolve to different levels as Darwinism implies (though they will likely deny this). The term race is, after all, an evolutionary term. The only race mentioned in the Bible is the human race (Malachi 2:10, Acts 17:26).

The biblical view is that all people are made in God's image.

So God created man in his own image, in the image of God created he him; male and female created he them. Genesis 1:27

The biblical view holds that all the genetic information found in humans today has been brought forth (descended) from the genetic data contained in the genomes of Noah and his immediate family which they had inherited from the genetic information God created in our original ancestors, Adam and Eve.

A 1995 study of the Y chromosome found in men indicated that all humans have descended from one man, known as the Y Chromosome Adam. Another study, this one of mitochondrial DNA found in women, revealed that humans can be traced back to one woman, known as the African or Mitochondrial Eve. Further research into mutation rates reveal Eve may have lived just 6,000 years ago! [112]

Though we have no idea what color the skin of Adam or Eve was, if two children from a pair of white and black couples were to eventually marry, their offspring could be any white, brown or black shade found among people around the globe.

As far as today's physical traits are concerned, following the Flood our genetic data was limited to the genetic information contained in the DNA of the four couples aboard Noah's ark. One researcher reported, *All humans come from one of four distinct gene pools.*[113]

Keep in mind that the biblical view holds that even people can bring forth variations within our kind due to the sorting (recombination) or loss (Gene Depletion) of the originally created genetic data. Due to the separation of people at the Tower of Babel, people groups spread out around the globe and brought forth from within their group's gene pool for a few thousand years. Slight variations accumulated in each group's DNA due to genetic losses caused by mutations and adaptations. These slight variations are the traits associated with any particular people group today.

The biblical view explains why we can do blood transfusions, kidney transplants and more between various looking people, as we did not evolve to different levels as Darwin implied in his worldview-altering book, *The Origin Of The Species By Means Of Natural Selection or The Preservation Of Favoured Races In The Struggle For Life.* 114

Yes, the secular crowd now hides the complete title of Darwin's book. But keep in mind that this evil philosophy holds that animals—Homo sapiens in our case—evolve to varying levels with the most evolved species winning the struggle for life.

The biblical interpretation is we didn't evolve into different races, our differences are only skin deep, and the earth was divided in the days of Peleg as people were separated by languages, nations, islands and continents.

History

Some of the surest evidence of the Truth of God's inspired Word comes from some of the most difficult sections to read through. I am referring to some of the genealogical records.

The biblical view is that human history goes back to Adam and Eve about 1,656 years before the global Flood. We know the approximate duration of the pre-Flood world because the chronologies in Genesis 5 cover the time from Adam to Noah.

The Hebrew translations of the root words in these genealogies can give several definitions which include:
- Adam – man
- Seth – appointed
- Enosh – mortal
- Kenan – sorrow
- Mahalalel – the blessed God
- Jared – shall come down
- Enoch – teaching
- Methuselah – his death shall bring (shall send)
- Lamech – the despairing
- Noah – comfort (rest)

Together these read: *Man is appointed mortal sorrow (but) the blessed God shall come down teaching. His death shall bring the despairing comfort (rest).*

Amazingly this is the message of the Christian Gospel in the first book of Scripture!

Because the Bible's chronologies run from Adam to Jesus, and because we know Jesus allowed Himself to be crucified about 2,000 years ago, we can arrive at an earth just a few thousand years old that endured a worldwide Flood about 4,400 to 4,500 years ago.

Human population studies agree with the biblical timeframe. Research shows that if there were only four couples in the world about 4,500 years ago, and if each of these four couples, and all couples since, averaged having 2.2 children, we would have about seven billion people on the earth today. Census reports say there are about seven billion people living on our planet. [115] Historical records also agree with the biblical timeframes. Written records only go back 4,700 to 5,000 years. These likely originated with Noah's family just prior to the Flood.

The secular view is that ancient man recorded lunar phases, built large stone (megalithic) structures, painted, made musical instruments and held religious ceremonies but failed to record their history for hundreds of thousands of years. [116]

The biblical interpretation is man was made in the beginning, has recorded history from the start, and that the world endured a global Flood 4,400 to 4,500 years ago.

Occam's Razor

"You blew me out of my chair when you spoke at my church. All my life I had questions about the relevance of Genesis in our 'scientific' world. God used you to bless my life in a most profound way."

Joe in AZ

Chapter Nineteen

Desolations in the Earth:
Mount St. Helens and Two Worldviews

Come, behold the works of the LORD, what desolations he hath made in the earth.

Psalm 46:8

If you have ever wanted to find evidence in support of the Bible, this chapter is for you.

God provided us with one of the most observed geological catastrophes in the history of the world at Mount St. Helens in the state of Washington on May 18, 1980 and during events taking place after the volcano's eruption. What was revealed at the volcanic site provided researchers with eyewitness proof that many of the earth's geological features, which geologists for the past 100 years have been taught required *millions of years to* occur, can actually form very quickly.

Allow me to provide the biblical and secular interpretations of the world's geology and compare both interpretations with information discovered at Mt. St. Helens.

Earth's outer crust

The biblical view of the earth's outer crust, which is primarily sedimentary layers of rock, is that the layers were laid down quickly by water during the worldwide Flood.

The secular view is based upon the belief that earth's outer crust of stratified sediments formed uniformly over long ages of time.

Mount St. Helens revealed three different methods by which finely stratified sedimentary layers could form in a matter of minutes or hours. First, a twenty-five foot thick layer of strata was laid down in a matter of minutes by flows that rushed from the volcano's crater at over 200 miles per hour. Second, air fall deposits formed finely stratified layers in a matter of days following the eruption as debris fell back to earth. In fact, in some locations, several hundred feet of finely stratified strata layers were laid down in a matter of minutes. Later, mud flows formed stratified layers in a matter of hours as an earthen dam that formed at the start of the eruption gave way and muddy water surged through the breached dam.

The gradual formation of sedimentary layers of rock over *millions of years* has never been observed. However, Secularists own the educational and scientific establishments. As a result, their view is taught as if it were scientific fact despite the overwhelming evidence that goes against their unobserved belief.

Lava flows

The biblical view of lava flows found among the sedimentary layers of the earth's outer crust is that the majority of these flows formed during the global Flood which caused the planet to endure massive tectonic plate activity. Because of the upheaval of the earth's crust toward the end of the Flood, post-Flood eruptions were much more common during the first thousand years following the Flood than they are today.

The secular view is that the radiometric dating techniques are accurate and that today's present rate of volcanism is the key to the earth's past rate of volcanic activity.

Mount St. Helens revealed that the radiometric dating of lava flows is completely unreliable. Rocks which were observed to have formed in the lava dome, since the eruption occurred, have been isotope dated as being up to 2,800,000 years old!

Coal layers

Note: Coal is often found in layers, with layers of rock strata separating the layers of coal. This is why coal is often extracted from the earth by strip mining. *Branching coal seams* are found that extend from the coal layer below, through the rock layer above, and into the upper layer of coal.

The biblical view of coal layers is that during the global Flood massive amounts of vegetation were uprooted and formed huge floating mats of organic debris, some more than 1,500 miles in diameter. Tree trunks were grinding against each other, crushing bark, limbs, leaves and other vegetation as the mats floated along on the flood waters. At the same time, saturated debris was sinking to the bottom to form future layers of coal. This organic material was quickly being covered by flowing sediments to form a layer of strata above the future layer of coal.

When the organic mats changed direction, due to winds or tides, they laid down additional layers of debris on top of the freshly deposited sediment layer to form today's coal layers that are separated by sedimentary layers of rock. At the point of the directional change, sinking plant matter got trapped within the sediment flow forming a future *branching coal seam* that extends from the coal layer below, through the rock layer above, and into the upper layer of coal.

The secular view is that coal layers form slowly over *millions of years* of time. They think that peat accumulated gradually in swamps and then, eventually, the region slowly uplifted and the swamp waters drained off, leaving the peat exposed so a layer of strata could slowly form on top of it. Millions of years later the area slowly sank back down allowing another swamp to form atop the strata layer. Secularists believe this scenario continued for *millions of years*, leaving behind the coal and rock layers that can be observed today.

The secular interpretation of *branching coal seams* is that the rock layer between the coal layers snapped, without breaking the fragile coal, and peat filled in the crack.

Mount St. Helens revealed how coal layers can form quickly as a result of a catastrophic aqueous event. During the eruption, Spirit Lake was covered by trees that had been blown down. Afterward, as the trees floated on the water, the tree trunks ground against each other, crushing bark, limbs and leaves. As the saturated organic debris sank to the bottom it was soon covered by sediments flowing into the lake to form future layers of coal.

Additional note: The Scriptural view of the Carboniferous layer is that it formed during the global Flood about 4,500 years ago. The secular interpretation is that this layer formed about 250 million years ago. However, measurable amounts of C-14 should decay away in less than 100,000 years (See Carbon Dating in Chapter 2), yet coal taken from the Carboniferous layer still contains plenty of this element. This means that the Carboniferous layer can only be a few thousand years old.

Additionally, all coal samples tested, from each of the coal-bearing layers, are found to contain C-14. This is strong evidence in support of the view that the earth's rock strata, and the coal layers in them, formed within the past few thousand years.

Fossils

The biblical view of the fossils that are found buried in the earth's sedimentary layers of rock is that they were drowned and buried quickly during the global Flood.

The secular view has been that fossilization and petrification require long ages of time to occur.

Mount St. Helens revealed that stratified layers of rock filled with the fossilized remains of plants and animals can form in just a few years of time. Finely stratified layers that formed as a result of the volcanic eruption have already hardened into rock.

These layers contain the remains of plants and animals that were victims of the catastrophic event.

Note: The plethora of items which are known to have petrified or fossilized in recent history is scientific proof that *millions of years* are not needed for these events to occur. Many secular-minded scientists now admit that both rocks and fossils can form very quickly under the right conditions

Fossils can form under various conditions, though water and dissolved minerals are usually required. Still, fossilization is somewhat rare today. [117] The billions of fossils in the strata layers fit perfectly with the biblical view of a world that has endured a global Flood which quickly buried plant and animal remains in sedimentary layers that were deposited by water.

Polystrate fossils

Note: *Polystrata*, or *polystrate*, fossils are fossils that extend through multiple layers of rock strata. *Polystrate* fossils of trees and fish are found in various layers of strata. Some *polystrate* trees have been found that are upside-down.

The biblical view of *polystrate* fossils is that during and after the global Flood, uprooted trees floated horizontally on the surface of the Flood waters, post-Flood seas, and post-Flood lakes. As the floating trees waterlogged, they became heavier and turned in an upright position, with the lighter end above the heavier end. Eventually, the upright floating log sank and floated against the bottom in the upright position. These logs, some upside-down, were then quickly buried by flowing sediments to become today's *polystrate* fossils. Due to the trees sinking at different times, the trunks can be found buried in various strata layers.

The secular view of *polystrate* fossils that traverse through several layers of strata is that a catastrophic event quickly buried a tree to form these interesting relics. Because they believe that strata form slowly over millions of years they assume the trees, found in various layers, grew at varying times and that the catastrophic events that formed them happened periodically over long ages of time.

Mount St. Helens revealed undeniable proof that *polystrate* fossils, as well as the layers they go through, form rapidly. During the eruption, nearby Spirit Lake was covered by trees that had been blown down. As these waterlogged, they turned and floated with the heavier end down prior to sinking to the bottom where they were buried by inflowing sediments while in the upright position. The bottom of nearby Spirit Lake is already littered with 50,000 to 55,000 *polystrate* tree trunks. Later, massive mud flows also produced *polystrate* fossils as well as multiple stratified layers.

Canyons

The biblical view of canyons is that the Flood waters were laying down sediment layers then eroding them away. The final time the Flood waters rushed off of the land masses they carved wide water channels and the majority of canyons we find today.

The secular view of canyons has held that they are carved out slowly and uniformly over unobserved *millions of years* of time.

Mount St. Helens revealed how canyons can form quickly as the result of surging water and mud flows. On March 19, 1982, an earthen dam that had formed during the eruption phase of the volcanic activity collapsed. The massive flow of water and mud that resulted from the dam's collapse carved a canyon more than a mile long, 160 feet deep and 1,000 feet wide in a matter of hours.

Taking **a Scriptural interpretation** of the evidence reveals God's uncompromised Word perfectly fits the scientifically observable facts. Meanwhile, the secular view is beginning to crumble due to the actual observation of the rapid formation of various canyons during massive water flow events.

It is hard to argue with observable events, and God provided mankind with one of the most observed geological catastrophes in the history of the world at Mount St. Helens. God used this relatively small volcano to reveal that the formation of strata layers, coal layers, canyons, fossils and more do not require *millions or billions of years* of time as secular science has been erroneously teaching for the past hundred years.

Once again, real science proves itself to be a Believer's true friend as observable facts reveal *billions of years of death before Adam* beliefs are an illusion, and that we can place our faith in the non-compromised Word of God.

"I had been a Gap Theorist until I read your book while on a cross-country flight. Then, at 33,000 feet, I saw the importance of the issues and accepted God's version of His creation."

Pastor G. Scott

"I believe in Christianity in the same way as I believe that the sun has risen. Not because I see it, but that by it, I see everything else."

C.S. Lewis

Chapter Twenty

The Global Flood: The Key to Earth's Geologic Past: Imagine the Global Deluge and Its Effects

The global Flood erodes old-earth beliefs, making it the lynch pin in the war of worldviews.

Russ Miller

Everyone loves a good mystery. In Genesis 1, God announced that days 1, 3, 4, and 5 were *good*, and at the end of the sixth and final day of Creation, He deemed that His Creation was *very good*. However, God did not refer to the second day as good.

So what is up with the second day? We can only speculate since God does not tell us. I am going to propose that this may have been because God made the fountains of the deep on the second day. God knew that He would eventually use the waters in those deep underground reservoirs to destroy His Creation during His judgment of mankind's sin.

Let's try to imagine the scene during the days of Noah. In our book, *371 Days That Scarred Our Planet*, Jim Dobkins and I penned a chapter describing some of the effects of the global Flood. We tried to provide a mental image of the catastrophe, even though we knew it was beyond what could be described. Building upon that description, please allow me to attempt to describe an event that is truly beyond human comprehension. 118

My goal is not to prove how God's global Flood judgment occurred. After all, God only gives us a few glimpses in Scripture. However it is vital to note that the critical question of how earth's strata layers formed is the key to one's belief in the age of the earth, when sin and death entered God's Creation, and for billions of people, whether or not they trust God's plan of salvation through our Lord and Savior Jesus Christ. Therefore, my aim is to use this imaginative exercise to show how having an understanding of God's catastrophic aqueous judgment is necessary in order to correctly interpret the massive evidences left behind by the event.

Start by imagining the world that was. Envision the huge land mass which had not yet broken up into multiple continents. Smell the lush, fruit-laden vegetation covering the land kept green by an amazing underground watering system that allows a mist to rise up and water the face of the ground.

...there went up a mist from the earth, and watered the whole face of the ground. Genesis 2:6

It is like living in a greenhouse; the climate is always mild. It is the perfect environment to allow people to live to incredible ages even after Adam's sin corrupted the Creation. No one has skin cancer from too much exposure to the sun's ultraviolet, gamma and x-rays as the mist and strong magnetic field protect the planet from many of the harmful cosmic rays.

Notice how man continues to rebel. In Genesis 6, we learn that the once-perfect world is now choked with violence and corruption.

13 *And God said unto Noah, The end of all flesh is come before me; for the earth is filled with violence through them; and, behold, I will destroy them with the earth.*

Know that God's judgment is coming. Yet, God will provide one plan of salvation for anyone who trusts in Him—the ark. And we learn there will be one way to enter into God's plan of salvation:

16*...and the door of the ark shalt thou set in the side thereof...*

Despite mankind's rebellion against Him, God will provide a narrow plank way that will lead through the ark's one door, His plan of salvation from the coming judgment for those who place their faith in Him. Noah and his family will do so.

Make thee an ark of gopher wood; rooms shalt thou make in the ark, and shalt pitch it within and without with pitch. Genesis 6:14

Listen and hear the sounds as Noah and his family prepare the ark, chopping trees, sawing planks, sanding wood, hammering nails, drilling holes, fitting wood beams into place, brushes slapping pitch onto the gopher wood, and ox-drawn wagons hauling bales of food onto the ark.

By faith Noah, being warned of God of things not seen as yet, moved with fear, prepared an ark to the saving of his house; by the which he condemned the world, and became heir of the righteousness which is by faith. Hebrews 11:7

Hear the skeptics scoff at Noah and his family. Hear the doubters question Noah's sanity and listen as the non-Believers curse. Little do they realize they are soon to be judged due to their sin. They do not understand that a watery grave awaits them.

Everyone has been invited to walk up the one narrow plank way that leads through the one door to salvation inside of the ark, yet see how the millions of people on the earth are eating, drinking and marrying while ignoring the Word of God. They are ignoring the witness of Noah. See that only Noah and his immediate family put their faith in God's plan.

Be a witness to the fact that no one will be able to say, *God gave me no warning*, as the building of the ark takes about 120 years to complete. Every nail, every plank, every action of Noah and his family are an outreach saying, *here is God's plan of salvation from the aqueous destruction to come.*

Observe as the animals, two by two, move up the narrow plank way and disappear into the ark. Seven of the clean animals follow them inside.

Of fowls after their kind, and of cattle after their kind, of every creeping thing of the earth after his kind, two of every sort shall come unto thee, to keep them alive. Genesis 6:20

See Noah and his family walk up the narrow plank way and disappear into the ark. Feel a chill run down your spine as you watch the plank way fall from the ark as the door mysteriously closes as if shut by the invisible hand of God.

And the LORD said unto Noah, Come thou and all thy house into the ark... 16 And they that went in...as God had commanded him: and the LORD shut him in. Genesis 7:1

Peer into the ark and see how Noah and his family are safely and comfortably nestled into their living quarters. All the provisions needed for their 371 days aboard the ark are stowed, and the animals are tucked into their pens, cages and roosts.

Suddenly, there is a rumbling noise and a slight tremor. It is initially so slight that you are not sure if it is actually there. But listen more intently as the sound grows louder. Suddenly, there is a sharp jolt followed by what feels like an earthquake. Then there are several earthquakes. The ground quivers as the fountains of the deep erupt around the globe.

In the six hundredth year of Noah's life, in the second month, the seventeenth day of the month, the same day were all the fountains of the great deep broken up, and the windows of heaven were opened. Genesis 7:11

Behold the surface of the earth split open violently and unexpectedly as the hot thermal waters from below the crust of the planet surge forth. See the scalding water, mixed with magma and hot mud, spew into the stratosphere from widening fissures that are suddenly ripping across the great mass of land.

Fact: The earth is crisscrossed by about 50,000 miles of fault lines many of which may be scars from where the fountains of the deep erupted.

Faces of horrified scoffers, which were so recently etched with sarcastic smirks, turn ashen. Too late they grasp the fact that they stood by, cursing the people who had placed their faith in the Word of God and built the ark in which they now floated safely above the rising muck and mire. Too late non-Believers, skeptics and scoffers realize that Noah was right, and that the time to receive God's plan for their salvation has passed.

And the waters prevailed, and were increased greatly upon the earth; and the ark went upon the face of the waters.
Genesis 7:18

Hear the anguished screams of men, women and children as they scramble to higher and higher ground for safety, some now pleading for Noah to reopen the door of the ark. Witness their houses, material goods and the temples to their false gods destroyed by the crushing weight of the flowing waters. And the water is relentless. It keeps rising.

Notice how the surging fountain waters erode massive amounts of soil along the edges of the cracks, producing a tremendous flow of muddy water. The animals living at the bottom of the sea, such as trilobites, are the first things covered by the flowing sediments.

The surging flows also drown all the poor creatures in their path, quickly burying them in the sedimentary layers of mud that are being laid down by the muddy water flow.

Fact: The magnetic field blocks harmful cosmic rays from destroying life on earth. [119] Evidence of rapid magnetic field reversals occurring during the global Flood was caught in molten magma being displaced by the erupting fountains of the deep. Since the catastrophic year-long Flood ended, the magnetic field has declined at a steady rate. Studies show that the total energy stored in the earth's magnetic field is decaying at a rate that only allows it to be a maximum of 20,000 years old.

Feel the scalding hot thermal waters warm the seas and observe the massive evaporation produce heavy cloud cover. View the skies as they abruptly change from blue to grey. Watch the rain fall, for the first time in earth's history, over the central regions of the globe as snows begin to encompass the poles.

Hear people continue to shriek for Noah to reopen the door into the ark. But Noah cannot provide them with salvation; only God can do that, and they rejected God's way. Now it is too late for them to enter into God's plan for salvation.

And spared not the old world, but saved Noah the eight person a preacher of righteousness bringing in the flood upon the world of the ungodly. 2 Peter 2:5

Watch people and wild animals run to and fro to no avail. No one can escape the catastrophic events that are unfolding. Some of their tracks, including those of dinosaurs, are covered by sediments to be preserved as proof of God's global judgment of man's sin.

Fact: Perfectly normal human footprints, such as the Laetoli track way, and amphibian, bird and dinosaur tracks have been found in deep strata layers. [120]

See God's windows of heaven rain down. Hear the birds and flying reptiles screech as landing places are covered with water. Look up and see their wings give out as they drop from the sky. See that the rain has been joined by hail. Initially, the icy pellets are the size of green peas, but the balls of ice steadily grow larger until they are the size of beach balls that pelt the earth and club victims into unconsciousness.

Witness people, cattle and creeping things being pounded into heaps of fur, meat and blood by the falling debris. See the ever-increasing waves erase dinosaurs and entire herds of frightened animals, then quickly bury them to be preserved as fossils.

See puffs of blood momentarily cloud the surface of the waters as the last surviving animals and people are eaten alive by huge sea creatures, such as masosaurs and giant sharks.

Fact: Researchers have discovered Carbon-14, which should decay in less than 100,000 years, in masosaur soft tissue remains.

Drink in the fading screams of people being carried off by the cascading, sediment-filled waters. Hear the deafening silence that is punctuated by the intensity of the crashing rainfall and the crushing thumps of the falling hail. Sense the sky as it turns from grey to charcoal. Feel the ground continue to shake violently.

Envision the huge walls of water as they crash down upon the earth. It's a scene of death, destruction and burial. There had only been one way to survive the turbulent deluge, and that one way was now closed. All people could do now was try to delay their eternal fate. It is a scene of total and complete judgment.

And, behold, I, even I, do bring a flood of waters upon the earth, to destroy all flesh, wherein is the breath of life, from under heaven; and every thing that is in the earth shall die. Genesis 6:17

The last of the condemned humans gasp for air as they struggle to keep from drowning, but weakened bodies slip below the waves or splinter on craggy rocks under the unimaginable crush of water and sediments. Some people survive for a few long and torturous days, but eventually all who were not on the ark succumb to the rising flood waters.

These are the people who rejected God's plan of salvation from the coming judgment. Each person could have walked up that narrow plank way and through the one door leading into the ark. But they chose to turn their back on their Creator, scoffing at Noah's efforts to warn them that their righteous heavenly Father was about to judge sin with waters that would cover all the high hills under the whole heaven.

And the waters prevailed exceedingly upon the earth; and all the high hills, that were under the whole heaven, were covered. Genesis 7:19

Watch as the rising waters overwhelm the planet. It is not a slow, steady rise. It is furious, destructive and violent beyond human imagination. Observe as the dead bodies of various animals are caught in whirlpools and deposited together under layers of sediments, sometimes with the bones of the dead creatures tangled together.

Fact: Fossil graveyards are found in various strata layers around the world. These are small geological areas where many kinds of creatures have been quickly buried together.

Feel the anguish as the fountains of the deep continue to burst forth with scalding hot waters, magma and mud for 50 days, 100 days, 150 days! Will they ever stop?!

And the waters prevailed upon the earth an hundred and fifty days. Genesis 7:24

Eventually, the fountains ebb and the rainfall ceases. Still, the flooding continues for another 150 days.

Feel the jolt and hear the roar as large sections of the earth's original crust collapse into the now-emptied chambers that once held the fountains of the deep.

...the waters stood above the mountains. At thy rebuke they fled; at the voice of thy thunder they hasted away. They go up by the mountains; they go down by the valleys unto the place which thou hast founded for them. Psalm 104:6-8

"Oh, dear God!" you shout as the giant, single land mass slides apart along where the fountains of the deep had erupted, forming multiple continents. Feel the earth quake violently as the planet's crust is twisted apart or smashed together, thrusting mountains skyward while folding some of the mud layers at incredibly sharp angles.

Fact: The tops of the world's tallest mountains are littered with seashells, and folded—yet unbroken—strata layers are seen around the globe.

Look at the smoke and fiery plumes as thousands of volcanoes erupt around the world. See the meteor-like rocks shooting across the sky. God's judgment is a scene of destruction and unimaginable power, and of God's mercy and grace.

And God remembered Noah, and every living thing, and all the cattle that was with him in the ark: and God made a wind to pass over the earth, and the waters assuaged. Genesis 8:1

Hear the wind gush as our Creator and Judge makes a wind to pass over the earth. The Spirit of God may be hovering once again over the waters that are now totally covering the earth, just as His Spirit did on the first day of His Creation week.

Watch the waters slosh back and forth as massive tsunamis come and go with waves that are taller than a thirty-story building. Observe the water as it picks up billions of tons of debris and sediment and deposits stratified layers in its wake. Look at the bodies of creatures that will provide fossils so people in the future will have no excuse for rejecting the truth of God's Word.

Fact: Carbon-14, which should decay away to immeasurable amounts in less than 100,000 years, is found in organic material in all fossil-bearing stratified rock layers. [121]

Envision most of today's geologic features as they are carved out by the receding waters which are cascading off the continents for the last time. See the 120 mile-per-hour flows remove more than a mile-deep layer of the sediments in some regions while leaving behind huge canyons in other places. Watch as the judgment waters settle into the collapsed areas to form today's oceans.

Fact: Today, rivers and storms dump about 20 billion pounds of sediments into the seas annually while today's plate tectonic processes only remove a billion tons of debris. [123] At today's rate of accumulation, the amount of sediments on the sea floor would form in 12 million years; however, most of the sediments were dumped into the seas during the Flood.

Imagine what's happening underground. Land and ocean life that had recently been buried by the hot mud and water are already becoming fossils. Stalactites and stalagmites are rapidly forming within caves as moisture flows through the sediment-rich layers of mud. Massive amounts of vegetation are captured within the waterborne layers to provide the material for natural gas, oil and coal deposits. Diamonds are quickly forming under the intense heat and pressure of volcanic activity.

Fact: Samples of oil, natural gas, and diamonds from around the world still contain Carbon-14, which should decay away to immeasurable amounts in fewer than 100,000 years.

Observe Noah and his family worship God as they await His signal to begin anew in the world that, being overflowed with water, had perished.

Whereby the world that then was, being overflowed with water, perished. 2 Peter 3:6

Fact: There are about 1,200 minerals in the earth. The amount of many, and the rate at which they are accumulating, can be measured in today's oceans. Each shows an ocean too young to fit its secular age of 3 billion years. For example, each year the world's oceans gain about 375 million tons of salt due to river runoff and sodium leaching from land masses. At this rate, the waters could have gone from fresh water to our present saltwater in about 40 million years. 122 However, most of the minerals were dumped into the seas during the global Flood.

Visualize the globe. Allow the white ice caps and the blue seas to remind you of God's past and His coming judgments of sin.

Witness the fact that no one will be able to say in the future, *God gave me no warning*, as every strata layer, fossil, piece of coal, diamond ring or quart of oil is an outreach saying, *God has provided us with a narrow pathway that leads through His one and only door to salvation from His coming judgment—Jesus Christ.* Future generations will be without an excuse should they choose to deny God.

Scriptural accounts claim there was a Flood that overflowed the world. Though not a science book, if the Bible is true, geology should find evidence of a global, catastrophic, aqueous event. This would be reliable, empirical criteria in support of God's Word. If the observable evidences did not support these claims, Scripture would be refuted.

Facts: Real science supports the Bible. Biblical Creation is a religious-based theory which meets its predictions and is refutable. However, God's Word has never been refuted because His Word is true, word for word and cover to cover.

Unfortunately, the secular misinterpretation of Flood evidence has caused billions of people to reject their Creator and His plan of salvation from His coming judgment of sin.

The issue is much more than the age of our planet. The lynch pin in the war between the secular and biblical worldviews is, did *billions of years* of death bring mankind into existence, or did man's original sin bring death into existence?

The global Flood matters.

"Awesome teaching! You gave me the answers I've been looking for."
Aleena in CA

Section IV: What We Can Do

Chapter Twenty-One

Ten Things We Can Do

Realize this is a war for the eternal soul.

Russ Miller

Would you like to impact the world for the glory of the Lord Jesus? Then help rebuild the biblical foundations, which are laid down in Genesis 1 and 3, within the Christian community.

The acronym I use to represent the biblical foundations, found in the early chapters of Genesis, is the **COSt**: God's perfect **(C)**reation was corrupted by Adam's **(O)**riginal Sin which **(S)**eparated us from God (allowing death to enter the world) requiring that we be † (the Cross) redeemed with our loving Creator who became our redeeming Savior, Lord Jesus the Christ.

With so many Christian schools, colleges and seminaries teaching old-earth beliefs that place death in the world before man existed, undermining the foundations of the Gospel message, and with the majority of Christians holding a secular worldview, if change is to occur, it must begin with you, your family and your church family.

Here are ten simple but powerful actions that anyone can take.

Parents

Is teaching your family to hold a biblical worldview a top priority for you? If not, review your priorities! God's plan for families is perfect. Learn what the Bible says about being a husband, wife and parent. Then follow His outline to success.

Ask yourself: Do I hold a biblical worldview? Do I understand

Scripture? Do I believe God's Word is inerrant and authoritative? Can I explain and defend the Scriptural position on billions *of years leading to Darwinism*? If you answered "no" to any of these questions you are not alone!

Praise God there is an abundance of books and DVDs to help you learn good biblical *apologetics* (from the Greek word *apologia* which means a defense.) Christian apologetics provide answers to questions from true seekers, scoffers and skeptics. There are fun and educational DVDs supporting the biblical view from which your family can enjoy and learn. We need to develop the same attitude of the psalmist in Psalms 101:3

I will set no wicked thing before mine eyes: I hate the work of them that turn aside; it shall not cleave to me.

Be diligent. Know and approve of the television shows your family watches or shut the TV off. The same goes for movies and the Internet.

Find a Bible-believing church that stands firm on God's version of His Creation and Flood judgment, and support the God-honoring pastor who leads it. Key questions to ask the pastor and leadership (teachers, youth leaders and associate pastors will also influence your family) include:
- What do you think about the Creation versus evolution issues?
- What do you think about the global Flood?
- How often do you have a creation speaker share here?
- Does your Sunday school curriculum teach biblical apologetics (the defense of Scripture)?

Parents are the front line for teaching their children, and your church should be a center of wisdom, knowledge and learning that supports the biblical worldview.

Children

The primary influences on a child's development are the child's parents, and parents must realize this is a war for the eternal soul of their child. If the biblical worldview is absent at home, a child will absorb whatever worldview he or she is exposed to. Today, that will be the secular worldview based on billions *of years of death leading to mankind through a Darwinian process*.

A church's pastor and teachers are meant to assist the family, not take the parents' place. Though grandparents, relatives and friends are also influential in a child's development, the ultimate responsibility to train up children lies with the parents. We learn this Scriptural principle in Deuteronomy 6:6-7:

And these words, which I command thee this day, shall be in thine heart. And thou shalt teach them to thy children, and shalt talk of them when thou sittest in thine house, and when thou walkest by the way, and when thou liest down, and when thou riseth up...

More than entertainment, toys or other material goods, your children want your time and attention. Read biblically-based books to your kids. Sit down and watch God-honoring DVDs with them. Make sure they understand the **COS†** and why they can put their trust in God's entire Word. You will learn as they learn.

With young children, every moment is an opportunity to develop how they view the world they live in. You will be amazed at how teachable young children are. Long before kids can read they are absorbing ideas and information. Humanists understand this well. Cartoons, museums, movies, dinosaur books, National Parks and more indoctrinate children from a very early age in the Humanistic foundation of *billions of years leading to Darwinism*.

Don't underestimate a child's ability to understand the biblical foundations and the Creation versus Darwinian-evolution issues. When I share a Creation message with a church family, I encourage them to keep their children in the service. Though some information may be over their heads, they will grasp plenty from our teachings. This can lead to some great family discussions. I know this because the questions kids ask afterward reveal their attentiveness.

Make sure the Christian-based resources you get address the *billions of years* and *Darwinism* issues. Many Christian educational materials ignore the earthly things due to compromises with old-earth beliefs. This leaves dinosaurs, fossils, rocks and more to be explained to our children through the secular worldview, and that is the worldview they will end up with if you ignore this issue. As Proverbs 22 says,

6 *Train up a child in the way he should go; and when he is old he will not depart from it.*

Youth

As your children get older, help them find friends who hold a biblical worldview by seeking out families that hold Christian values. Peer acceptance and support are especially important for youth.

Address the key issues that will challenge your child's faith. Show them why secular teachings do not mesh with the best interpretations of observable facts. Then ensure they understand how properly interpreted evidence supports a recent Creation, and the overall biblical worldview.

CESM DVDs, audios and books are great ways to learn this information at a popular, easy to understand level. There are also many great creation family camps, trips, and conferences that offer an opportunity for the whole family to learn together. Great examples are our Grand Canyon Rim tours, and our trips through the Grand Staircase, which we began offering in 2004. These can be reviewed on our website.

And ye fathers, provoke not your children to wrath: but bring them up in the nurture and admonition of the Lord. Ephesians 6:4

Teachers

Leading a Sunday school, children's church, or youth group is a great ministry. This takes a lot of effort when done properly and can be very fruitful in helping both you and others grow in their knowledge of the Lord.

As an educator, you need to invest in your own personal learning to get a solid understanding of many topics, including good apologetics. Encourage your church to send you and other teachers to Worldview Conferences and lectures supporting biblical Creation and other foundational issues.

As a Christian educator, you could have a huge influence on the resources and curriculum your church uses in its educational programs. You could also lead the charge to get relevant speakers into your church to help train children and parents in the apologetics they need to develop and defend the biblical worldview.

Learn to teach *historical biblical accounts* rather than *Bible stories*. The Bible is not a book of fairy tales. It's the true history book of the universe through which we can correctly view the world. As an example, instead of saying, "We are going to read the story of King David" say, "We are going to study the history of King David." Teach the Bible is true and relevant for guiding your students' lives.

Christian Education: IT'S NOT JUST FOR CHILDREN.

The whole church, from cradle to grave, needs to be working toward strengthening their biblical worldview. Because iron sharpens iron, adult education classes and family courses need to cover the same type of information as the children's teachings do so all church members can hold a biblical view and learn to defend their faith.

Youth and College Pastors

Youth and college pastors who stand firm on the non-compromised Word of God have my greatest respect. The young minds that youth or college pastors work with have been bombarded with *billions of years leading to Darwinism* teachings for most of their lives.

Youth and college pastors are usually hired to *relate* to their group, and unfortunately, whether or not they are considered to be successful is based on the answer to one question: How many kids attended last night's meeting?

This is a huge mistake as it pressures the pastor to avoid issues that matter in a young person's life and only present seeker-friendly lessons. This is because relevant issues tend to be controversial and may upset someone who does not agree with the Scriptural position.

However, as a youth or college pastor, to ignore these issues turns you into a babysitter when your group needs a Christian leader. To be a leader requires that you teach the biblical view on key, relevant issues such as Creation versus evolution, abortion, and pre-marital sex. Read John 10:11-13 and choose to be a shepherd. Build their faith on the biblical foundations, the **COS†**.

Senior Pastors

For this cause also thank we God without ceasing, because, when ye received the word of God which ye heard of us, ye received it not as the word of men, but as it is in truth, the word of God, which effectually worketh also in you that believe. 1 Thessalonians 2:13

Man-made formulas tend to be successful from a worldly standpoint of building larger businesses and have created what I call the Christian Industry. Set the foundation of your church on the Rock, the uncompromised Word of God. Everyone in your flock is constantly inundated with the secular view, evolution and *billions of years* beliefs. Let your preaching equip your flock with rock-solid biblical truths. Ensure that your church family understands the **COS†** and why they can believe the Bible's foundations, even providing the evidence needed for your flock to defend their biblical worldview in our secular society.

A pastor has to be knowledgeable in an incredibly wide range of issues, and no one can be an expert in them all. Thankfully, God has provided many God-honoring specialists to assist in specific areas, especially in apologetics.

As the church leader, make sure all staff members, elders, deacons, trustees and teachers understand the foundational issues and hold a biblical worldview. If they do not, lovingly explain why we need to accept God's Word and offer them supporting resources. Classes, DVDs, conferences, speakers, seminars, books, tapes and more are at your disposal.

Unfortunately, with the majority of Christians now holding a secular worldview, someone may get upset. Still, you are the one called to shepherd your flock, so do not allow anyone to threaten or undermine your ministry. As a last resort, and in order to protect your flock, you may have to say goodbye to someone.

Russ, I was teaching about Noah's Ark and the global Flood in Sunday school when our church's leaders came in and forbid us to teach on these things. Tom

Until this situation is rectified, the Christian Church and Scripturally-based teachings will continue to be seen as irrelevant in the eyes of the world.

Field Trips, Family Trips and Vacations

One of the best teaching tools for biblical Creation is God's Creation. As Bible-believing Christians, we need to take advantage of creation-based trips that study God's Word in light of the earth we live on. Seeing our planet through a biblical view makes the Bible come alive as folks realize its relevance to the world we live in and to their very own lives.

I lead Grand Canyon Rim tours, Grand Staircase trips and

Colorado River rafting adventures all based on the God- honoring interpretation of this Flood-devastated region. These trips are eye-opening and fun. There are many other creation-based museums, camps, fossil digs and hikes around the world that also reveal the Truth of the Bible. And tons of information can be found on DVDs and in books. Take advantage of these resources!

Make This Your DVD Ministry!

I wanted to provide people with an opportunity to run a life-changing, soul-saving ministry that would not require years of study or spending thousands of dollars to start and operate; in fact, it needed to be very inexpensive to run and easy for anyone to do.

I asked God how to accomplish this, and He led me to allow people to *copy and give away* my DVDs. So I encourage everyone who gets our DVDs to give away copies to family, friends, church members...to whomever they choose. Hand them out at a county fair, on a college campus or wherever you feel led. It's a grassroots effort that God is using to change lives and reap a bountiful harvest of saved souls. In Matthew 9 Jesus told His disciples,

37-38 ...The harvest truly is plenteous, but the labourers are few; Pray ye therefore the Lord of the harvest, that he will send forth labourers into his harvest.

Evangelize Like an Apostle

In today's multi-cultural society, sowing the seed, the Gospel of Jesus Christ, can be a challenge. To effectively evangelize people with a wide range of beliefs, I suggest we learn from the great apostle Paul.

When speaking with Jews, who held a Creation-based foundation and understood the **COS†**, Paul simply told them Jesus was the redeeming Messiah who had died for their sins. A bountiful harvest of saved souls was reaped. However, Paul also reported that preaching Christ crucified was foolishness to the Greeks (1 Corinthians 1). This was because the Greeks did not have a Creation-based foundation. They did not understand the **COS†**, that Adam's original sin had corrupted God's perfect Creation, separating us from our loving Creator, requiring our redemption with Him.

In Acts 17 we learn the great apostle regrouped and became a Creation evangelist, telling the Greeks their unknown god was He who had made the world and all things therein. Paul showed us that people must first understand that we have a Creator and why mankind needs to be reconciled with Him before they can logically receive the good news of our redeeming Savior, Lord Jesus the Christ. People need to understand the foundational accounts found in Genesis.

Today, we live in a society which has accepted the secular interpretation of the world and largely rejected the Bible's creation-based foundations, the **COS†**.

I would *guestimate* that even 95% of Christians do not understand the foundational issues established in Genesis 1 and 3. This lack of knowledge has caused many within the institutionalized church to think it is okay to deny Jesus is the Creator (six days) and Judge (global Flood) He claims to be.

Much worse than denying Jesus is who He claims to be, the loss of knowledge in the foundational issues has misled many Christians to accept non-biblical types of Christs. These various versions of Jesus are simply attempts to fit secular-based, *death before Adam* beliefs into God's Word and further erode people's faith in the foundational issues.

We are, in fact, preaching to the Greeks not only in our society, but often within the institutionalized church as well.

Creation evangelism prepares the soil for the planting of the seed by plowing up secular influences and rebuilding the biblical foundations. This provides reasons for the hope that is in the heart of all true seekers.

Incidentally, on the day of His resurrection, Jesus began teaching His disciples from Moses (Luke 24). Does this mean our Creator and Savior is a Creation evangelist?

What do you think?

"I had never considered what it did to the Gospel message if death existed before Adam's sin. Thanks for what you are doing!"

Aaron in IA

"Our Youth Group and Adult Sunday School have been going through your DVDs and everyone is finding them both interesting and informative. I've long been a believer in biblical creation but your messages have encouraged me to be even more assertive in sharing this information with others."

Pastor Dan in MI

"We have been reading your book in our Wednesday evening meetings and I wanted to let you know what a blessing it has been to all of us. I learned things I hadn't thought about before, important things that have even strengthened my faith."

Pastor Ken in KS

"I believed in biblical Creation before I met you but hearing what you shared made me the crusader for Creation that I am today."

Pastor Owen in OR

Chapter Twenty-Two

From Creation to Salvation
The COS†

Jesus Christ is our Creator, Judge, Savior and Coming King.

Russ Miller

We are told in John 1 that the Word of God is our Creator: *1 In the beginning was the Word... 3 All things were made by him...*

We are also told in John 1 that our Creator, the Word of God, is our Lord and Savior, Jesus Christ: 14 *And the Word was made flesh, and dwelt among us...*So Jesus is our Creator and He is the Word of God.

Jesus also called Himself the bread of life in John 6:35 *And Jesus said...I am the bread of life...* So Jesus is the Word of God, and He is the bread of life. Yet when tempted by Satan in Luke 4:4, Jesus told him*: ...man shall not live by bread alone, but by every word of God.*

Thus, Jesus Christ, the bread of life, by whom we are saved, is found in the uncompromised Word of God, starting with the first five words which read: *In the beginning God created...* Genesis 1:1a

My hope and prayer is that this book will help you put your faith in these first five words of the Bible and in every word that follows, word for word and cover to cover.

The Bible's message of salvation is simple: *We receive God's free gift of salvation through faith alone, in Jesus Christ alone.*

For God so loved the world, that he gave his only begotten Son, that whosoever believeth in him should not perish, but have everlasting life. John 3:16

We've all sinned against God (Romans 3:23) and because of our sin, we've earned God's judgment (Romans 6:23): spiritual death followed by physical death. There's nothing we can do on our own to make ourselves right with God, so out of love, our Creator became a human in the person of Jesus Christ.

In John 10:9 Jesus tells us: ***I am the door: by me if any man enter in, he shall be saved...***

However, as foretold in Scripture, man rejected Jesus and crucified Him. Jesus allowed this to occur so He could die in our place, accepting the punishment for our sin (2 Corinthians 5:21). Jesus then resurrected on the third day (1 Corinthians 15), overcoming death.

Through His grace, God offers us salvation from eternal death as a free gift when we believe our Creator, Jesus Christ, took on human form, made full payment for our sins (1 John 2:2) when He shed His blood and died on Calvary's cross, and defeated death by rising victorious from the grave three days later.

Jesus, our redeeming Savior, will return in the nearing future to take those of us who have placed our trust in Him home to live with Him in perfect peace and joy for all eternity.

I pray that you will accept this glorious truth today and place your trust in Him, and that He will change you just as He has changed me.

May God bless you.

Additional Notes

Thomas Jefferson's
Letter to the Danbury Baptist Association of Connecticut
Written October, 7, 1801

Gentlemen

The affectionate sentiments of esteem and approbation which you are so good as to express towards me, on behalf of the Danbury Baptist association, give me the highest satisfaction. My duties dictate a faithful and zealous pursuit of the interests of my constituents, and in proportion as they are persuaded of my fidelity to those duties, the discharge of them becomes more and more pleasing.

Believing with you that religion is a matter which lies solely between Man and his God, that he owes account to none other for his faith or his worship, that the legitimate powers of government reach actions only, and not opinions, I contemplate with sovereign reverence that act of the whole American people which declared that their legislature should "make no law respecting an establishment of religion, or prohibiting the free exercise thereof," thus building a wall of separation between church and state.

Adhering to this expression of the supreme will of the nation in behalf of the rights of conscience, I shall see with sincere satisfaction the progress of those sentiments which tend to restore to man all his natural rights, convinced he has no natural right in opposition to his social duties.

I reciprocate your kind prayers for the protection and blessing of the common father and creator of man, and tender you for yourselves and your religious association, assurances of my high respect and esteem.

Th Jefferson

Abraham Lincoln's
Second Inaugural Address
Delivered in Washington, D.C. on March 4, 1865

Fellow-Countrymen:

At this second appearing to take the oath of the Presidential office there is less occasion for an extended address than there was at the first. Then a statement somewhat in detail of a course to be pursued seemed fitting and proper. Now, at the expiration of four years, during which public declarations have been constantly called forth on every point and phase of the great contest which still absorbs the attention and engrosses the energies of the nation, little that is new could be presented. The progress of our arms, upon which all else chiefly depends, is as well known to the public as to myself, and it is, I trust, reasonably satisfactory and encouraging to all. With high hope for the future, no prediction in regard to it is ventured.

On the occasion corresponding to this four years ago all thoughts were anxiously directed to an impending civil war. All dreaded it, all sought to avert it. While the inaugural address was being delivered from this place, devoted altogether to saving the Union without war, insurgent agents were in the city seeking to destroy it without war--seeking to dissolve the Union and divide effects by negotiation. Both parties deprecated war, but one of them would make war rather than let the nation survive, and the other would accept war rather than let it perish, and the war came.

One-eighth of the whole population were colored slaves, not distributed generally over the Union, but localized in the southern part of it. These slaves constituted a peculiar and powerful interest. All knew that this interest was somehow the cause of the war. To strengthen, perpetuate, and extend this interest was the object for which the insurgents would rend the Union even by war, while the Government claimed no right to do more than to restrict the territorial enlargement of it. Neither party expected for the war the magnitude or the duration which it has already attained. Neither anticipated that the cause of the conflict might cease with or even before the conflict itself should cease. Each looked for an easier triumph, and a result less fundamental and astounding. Both read the same Bible and pray to the same God, and each invokes His aid against the other. It may seem strange that any men should dare to ask a just God's assistance in wringing their bread from the sweat of other men's faces, but let us judge not, that we be not judged. The prayers of both could not be answered. That of neither has been answered fully. The Almighty has His own purposes. "Woe unto the world because of offenses; for it must needs be that offenses come, but woe to that man by whom the offense cometh." If we shall suppose that American slavery is one of those offenses which, in the providence of God, must needs come, but which, having continued through His appointed time, He now wills to remove, and that He gives to both North and South this terrible war as the woe due to those by whom the offense came, shall we discern therein any departure from those divine attributes which the believers in a living God always ascribe to Him? Fondly do we hope, fervently do we pray, that this mighty scourge of war may speedily pass away. Yet, if God wills that it continue until all the wealth piled by the bondsman's two hundred and fifty years of unrequited toil shall be sunk, and until every drop of blood drawn with the lash shall be paid by another drawn with the sword, as was said three thousand years ago, so still it must be said "the judgments of the Lord are true and righteous altogether."

With malice toward none, with charity for all, with firmness in the right as God gives us to see the right, let us strive on to finish the work we are in, to bind up the nation's wounds, to care for him who shall have borne the battle and for his widow and his orphan, to do all which may achieve and cherish a just and lasting peace among ourselves and with all nations.

Martin Luther King, Jr's "I Have a Dream" Speech
Delivered from the steps of the Lincoln Memorial in Washington, D.C. on August 28, 1963

I am happy to join with you today in what will go down in history as the greatest demonstration for freedom in the history of our nation.

Five score years ago, a great American, in whose symbolic shadow we stand today, signed the Emancipation Proclamation. This momentous decree came as a great beacon light of hope to millions of Negro slaves who had been seared in the flames of withering injustice. It came as a joyous daybreak to end the long night of their captivity.

But one hundred years later, the Negro still is not free. One hundred years later, the life of the Negro is still sadly crippled by the manacles of segregation and the chains of discrimination. One hundred years later, the Negro lives on a lonely island of poverty in the midst of a vast ocean of material prosperity. One hundred years later, the Negro is still languished in the corners of American society and finds himself an exile in his own land. And so we've come here today to dramatize a shameful condition.

In a sense we've come to our nation's capital to cash a check. When the architects of our republic wrote the magnificent words of the Constitution and the Declaration of Independence, they were signing a promissory note to which every American was to fall heir. This note was a promise that all men, yes, black men as well as white men, would be guaranteed the "unalienable Rights" of "Life, Liberty and the pursuit of Happiness."

It is obvious today that America has defaulted on this promissory note, insofar as her citizens of color are concerned. Instead of honoring this sacred obligation, America has given the Negro people a bad check, a check which has come back marked "insufficient funds."

But we refuse to believe that the bank of justice is bankrupt. We refuse to believe that there are insufficient funds in the great vaults of opportunity of this nation. And so, we've come to cash this check, a check that will give us upon demand the riches of freedom and the security of justice.

We have also come to this hallowed spot to remind America of the fierce urgency of Now. This is no time to engage in the luxury of cooling off or to take the tranquilizing drug of gradualism. Now is the time to make real the promises of democracy. Now is the time to rise from the dark and desolate valley of segregation to the sunlit path of racial justice. Now is the time to lift our nation from the quicksands of racial injustice to the solid rock of brotherhood. Now is the time to make justice a reality for all of God's children.

It would be fatal for the nation to overlook the urgency of the moment. This sweltering summer of the Negro's legitimate discontent will not pass until there is an invigorating autumn of freedom and equality. 1963 is not an end, but a beginning. And those who hope that the Negro needed to blow off steam and will now be content will have a rude awakening if the nation returns to business as usual. And there will be neither rest nor tranquility in America until the Negro is granted his citizenship rights. The whirlwinds of revolt will continue to shake the foundations of our nation until the bright day of justice emerges.

But there is something that I must say to my people, who stand on the warm threshold which leads into the palace of justice: In the process of gaining our rightful place, we must not be guilty of wrongful deeds. Let us not seek to satisfy our thirst for freedom by drinking from the cup of bitterness and hatred. We must forever conduct our struggle on the high plane of dignity and discipline. We must not allow our creative protest to degenerate into physical violence. Again and again, we must rise to the majestic heights of meeting physical force with soul force.

The marvelous new militancy which has engulfed the Negro community must not lead us to a distrust of all white people, for many of our white brothers, as evidenced by their presence here today, have come to realize that their destiny is tied up with our destiny. And they have come to realize that their freedom is inextricably bound to our freedom.

We cannot walk alone. And as we walk, we must make the pledge that we shall always march ahead. We cannot turn back.

There are those who are asking the devotees of civil rights, "When will you be satisfied?" We can never be satisfied as long as the Negro is the victim of the unspeakable horrors of police brutality.

We can never be satisfied as long as our bodies, heavy with the fatigue of travel, cannot gain lodging in the motels of the highways and the hotels of the cities.

We cannot be satisfied as long as the negro's basic mobility is from a smaller ghetto to a larger one. We can never be satisfied as long as our children are stripped of their self-hood and robbed of their dignity by a sign stating: "For Whites Only."

We cannot be satisfied as long as a Negro in Mississippi cannot vote and a Negro in New York believes he has nothing for which to vote. No, no, we are not satisfied, and we will not be satisfied until "justice rolls down like waters, and righteousness like a mighty stream."

I am not unmindful that some of you have come here out of great trials and tribulations. Some of you have come fresh from narrow jail cells. And some of you have come from areas where your quest -- quest for freedom left you battered by the storms of persecution and staggered by the winds of police brutality. You have been the veterans of creative suffering. Continue to work with the faith that unearned suffering is redemptive. Go back to Mississippi, go back to Alabama, go back to South Carolina, go back to Georgia, go back to Louisiana, go back to the slums and ghettos of our northern cities, knowing that somehow this situation can and will be changed.

Let us not wallow in the valley of despair, I say to you today, my friends.

And so even though we face the difficulties of today and tomorrow, I still have a dream. It is a dream deeply rooted in the American dream.

I have a dream that one day this nation will rise up and live out the true meaning of its creed: "We hold these truths to be self-evident, that all men are created equal."

I have a dream that one day on the red hills of Georgia, the sons of former slaves and the sons of former slave owners will be able to sit down together at the table of brotherhood.

I have a dream that one day even the state of Mississippi, a state sweltering with the heat of injustice, sweltering with the heat of oppression, will be transformed into an oasis of freedom and justice.

I have a dream that my four little children will one day live in a nation where they will not be judged by the color of their skin but by the content of their character.

I have a *dream* today! I have a dream that one day, down in Alabama, with its vicious racists, with its governor having his lips dripping with the words of "interposition" and "nullification" -- one day right there in Alabama little black boys and black girls will be able to join hands with little white boys and white girls as sisters and brothers.

I have a *dream* today! I have a dream that one day every valley shall be exalted, and every hill and mountain shall be made low, the rough places will be made plain, and the crooked places will be made straight; "and the glory of the Lord shall be revealed and all flesh shall see it together."

This is our hope, and this is the faith that I go back to the South with.

With this faith, we will be able to hew out of the mountain of despair a stone of hope. With this faith, we will be able to transform the jangling discords of our nation into a beautiful symphony of brotherhood. With this faith, we will be able to work together, to pray together, to struggle together, to go to jail together, to stand up for freedom together, knowing that we will be free one day.

And this will be the day -- this will be the day when all of God's children will be able to sing with new meaning:

> *My country 'tis of thee, sweet land of liberty, of thee I*
> *sing. Land where my fathers died, land of the Pilgrim's*
> *pride, From every mountainside, let freedom ring!*

And if America is to be a great nation, this must become true. And so let freedom ring from the prodigious hilltops of New Hampshire. Let freedom ring from the mighty mountains of New York. Let freedom ring from the heightening Alleghenies of Pennsylvania. Let freedom ring from the snow-capped Rockies of Colorado. Let freedom ring from the curvaceous slopes of California.

But not only that: Let freedom ring from Stone Mountain of Georgia. Let freedom ring from Lookout Mountain of Tennessee. Let freedom ring from every hill and molehill of Mississippi. From every mountainside, let freedom ring.

And when this happens, when we allow freedom ring, when we let it ring from every village and every hamlet, from every state and every city, we will be able to speed up that day when all of God's children, black men and white men, Jews and Gentiles, Protestants and Catholics, will be able to join hands and sing in the words of the old Negro spiritual:

> *Free at last! Free at last!*
> *Thank God Almighty, we are free at last!*

Join us on YouTube, Facebook, Twitter, GodTube, Vimeo and more.

Visit our website to:
- watch CESM videos
- review our Grand Canyon Rim tours
- Learn of our Grand Staircase tours
- see our other books, DVDs and resources
- find Russ' speaking schedule
- and much more

www.CreationMinistries.Org

References

1. New Scientist; May 22, 2004.

2. Sir F. Hoyle; C. Wickramasinghe; Evolution from Space; 1981; Pg 135.

3. CESM presentation: 50 Facts Compared to God's Word; STM version; 2008; visuals 30-34.

4. Dr. Bergman, J., Perspectives on Science and Christian Faith; September; 1994.

5. CESM presentation: An Old Earth or A Global Flood, 2008; visual 58.

6. Thomas, B., M.S.; Radioactive Decay Rates Not Stable; August 5, 2009; http://www.icr.org/article/radioactive-   decay-rates-not-stable/.

7. Miller, R., Dobkins, J., 371 Days That Scarred Our Planet; 2009; pg 80.

8. CESM presentation: An Old Earth or a Global Flood; and J Moore; Teaching About Origins Questions: Origin of Human Beings; Creation Research Society; March 1986; page 185.

9. Riddle, Mike, Doesn't Carbon-14 Dating Disprove the Bible?; 9-20-07; www.answersingenesis.org/articles/nab/does-c14-disprove-the-bible.

10. Dr. Baumgardner, J., Measurable 14-C in fossilized organic materials; Proceedings of the Fifth International Conference on Creationism; Vol. II; 2003; Creation Science Fellowship; Pittsburgh, PA; pages 127–142.

11. Carbon Dating Undercuts Evolution's Long Ages; J. Baumgardner, Ph.D. http://www.icr.org/articles/view/117/262/.

12. CESM presentation: An Old Earth or A Global Flood; 2008; visual 92.

13. Miller, R., CreationMinistries.Org's Noah's Ark & Dinosaurs Coloring Book; 2012; page 8.

14. Gentry, R., W. Christie, D. Smith, J. Emery, S. Reynolds, R. Walker, S. Christy, and P. Gentry; Radiohalos in coalified wood: new evidence relating to time of uranium introduction and coalification; Science 194:315–318; October 15, 1976; Section 2.

15. Vail, T., Oard, M., Bokovoy, D., Hergenrather, J.; Your Guide to the Grand Canyon; 2008; page 156.

16. National Geographic for Kids; page 5; March, 2005.

17. Dinosaurs By Design; Dr. D Gish; page 23; 1992.

18. Dinosaurs By Design; Dr. D Gish; page 23; 1992.

19. Abusing Science: The Case Against Creationism; Philip Kitcher; 1998, page 121.

20. Miller, R., CreationMinistries.Org's Noah's Ark & Dinosaurs Coloring Book; 2012; page 14.

21. DG Lindsay; The Birth of Planet Earth & the age of the Universe; 1993; pages 18-20.

22. Schweitzer, Wittmeyer, Horner and Toporski; Soft-Tissue vessels and cellular preservation in T rex; Science 207:1952–1955; 3-25-2005.

23. Miller, R., CreationMinistries.Org's Noah's Ark & Dinosaurs Coloring Book; 2012; page 15.

24. Dr. Bergman, Jerry; Abiogenesis Is Impossible; 1999; Creation Research Society Quarterly; Vol. 36; No. 4.

25. Evolution vs. Creationism; U of CA Press; E.C. Scott; 2009; page 26.

26. Miller, R., Dobkins, J., The Darwinian Delusion; 2010; pages 90-91.

27. CESM presentation: 50 Facts versus Darwinism in the Textbooks; 2006, visual #'s 31-32.

28. CESM presentation: 50 Facts versus Darwinism in the Textbooks; 2006; visual # 7.

29. Miller, R., Dobkins, J., The Darwinian Delusion; 2010; pages 88-89.

30. CESM presentation: 50 Facts versus Darwinism in the Textbooks; visual #'s 35-44.

31. CESM presentation: 80 Facts versus Darwinism; 2007: visuals 112-113.

32. C. Darwin; The Origin of Species by Means of Natural Selection or The Preservation of Favored Races in the Struggle for Life; 1859; pg 170.

33. Miller, R., Dobkins, J., The Darwinian Delusion; 2010; pages 132-134.

34. Miller, R., Dobkins, J., The Darwinian Delusion; 2010; page 131.

35. CESM presentation: 80 Facts versus Darwinism; 2007: visuals 85-86.

36. CESM presentation: 80 Facts versus Darwinism; 2007: visuals 87-89.

37. CESM presentation: 50 Facts versus Darwinism in the Textbooks, 2006; visual #'s 48-50.

38. CESM presentation: 50 Facts versus Darwinism in the Textbooks, 2006, visual # 51.

39. J Ross, Chemical and Engineering News, July 27, 1980, page 40.

40. Glenco Biology; 1998; page 324.

41. Glenco Biology; 1998; page 324.

42. CESM presentation: 50 Facts versus Darwinism in the Textbooks: 2006: visual # 56.

43. Nature 463, 536-539; January 28, 2010.

44. CESM presentation: 50 Facts versus Darwinism in the Textbooks: 2006: visual #'s 57-58.

45. CESM presentation: 50 Facts versus Darwinism in the Textbooks: 2006: visual #'s 66-68.

46. C. Darwin; Origin of Species; 6th edition, 1872; London, J. Murray; 1902; page 413.

47. C. Darwin; The Origin of Species by Means of Natural Selection or the Preservation of Favored Races in the Struggle for Life; 1859 page 211.

48. CESM presentation: 80 Facts versus Darwinism; 2007: visuals 143-144.

49. CESM presentation: 50 Facts versus Darwinism in the Textbooks: 2006: visual # 74.

50. Miller, R., Dobkins, J., The Darwinian Delusion; 2010; pages 111-112.

51. Shubin, N. Daeschler, E. Jenkins, F., The pectoral fin of Tiktaalik roseae and the origin of the tetrapod limb; Nature 440; 764-771 doi:10.1038/nature04637; April 6, 2006.

52. C. Patterson, from a letter to Luther Sunderland, April 10, 1979, as published in Darwin's Enigma; Green fossil, AR: Master Books, 4th edition; 1988; page 89.

53. CESM presentation: 50 Facts versus Darwinism in the Textbooks: 2006: visual # 65.

54. S.J. Gould, Evolution Now: A Century After Darwin, John Maynard Smith, New York: Macmillan Publishing Co., 1982.

55. Juby, I., Ian's Science Notes; http://ianjuby.org/scinote_sept_2008.html.

56. Juby, I., Dinos to Birds; Nov 12, 2010 CrEvo News with Ian Juby and CORE Ottawa; http://ianjuby.org/ newsletter/?p=417#2.

57. The 'Missing Link' That Wasn't" by Tim Friend; USA TODAY; February 3, 2000.

58. Nature 322; 8-21-1986; Science 253; 7-5-1991.

59. Archaeopteryx; Nature 322; 8-21-1986; Science 253; 7-5-1991.

60. "Lucy" isn't the "Missing Link!"; Creation Magazine; June 1, 1990. http://www.answersingenesis.org/articles/ cm/v12/n3/lucy

61. Fossils, Teeth and Sex: New Perspectives on Human Evolution, Charles Oxnard, University of Washington Press, Seattle and London; 1987; page 227.

62. Miller, R., Dobkins, J., The Darwinian Delusion; 2010; pages 98-99.

63. CESM presentation: 50 Facts versus Darwinism in the Textbooks: 2006: visual # 91.

64. Biology; KR Miller and J Levine; Prentice Hall; 2006; page 838.

65. Science News; October, 2002; Volume 162 # 16; page 253.

66. Nature 66; October, 2002.

67. Biology; KR Miller; J Levine; Prentice Hall; 2006; page 838.

68. Watts, A., Scientists Unveil Missing Link In Evolution; Sky News; May 20, 2009,

69. Miller, R., Dobkins, J., The Darwinian Delusion; 2010; pages 103-104.

70. Miller, R., Dobkins, J., The Darwinian Delusion; 2010; pages 102-103.

71. J. Viegas; Discovery News; The Human Family Tree; discovery.com; 11-2010.

72. CESM presentation: 50 Facts versus Darwinism in the Textbooks: 2006: visual #'s 64-65.

73. Miller, R., Dobkins, J., The Facts Are Talking; 2008; page 109.

74. CESM presentation: 80 Facts versus Darwinism; 2007: visuals 65-71.

75. Miller, R., Dobkins, J., The Darwinian Delusion; 2010; pages 129-131.

76. Teachers Guidebook; National Academy of Sciences; 1998; pgs 16-17.

77. Miller, R., Dobkins, J., The Darwinian Delusion; 2010; pages 125-127.

78. Miller, R., Dobkins, J., The Darwinian Delusion; 2010; pages 76-77.

79. Bergman, J., Journal of Creation; Volume 25; Issue 2; fall 2011; The chromosome 2 fusion model of evolution: re-evaluating the evidence.

80. CESM presentation: 50 Facts versus Darwinism in the Textbooks: 2006: visual #'s 53-55.

81. The Times; London, UK; August 11, 1997; page 14.

82. CESM presentation: 80 Facts versus Darwinism; 2007: visuals 107-111.

83. Pascal Lectures; University of Waterloo; Ontario, Canada.

84. Darwin, C., The Origin of Species by Means of Natural Selection or the Preservation of Favored Races in the Struggle for Life; 1859; and My Life and Letters; Volume 1.

85. F. Galton, Hereditary talent and character; MacMillan; 12:157-166 & 316-328, June-August, 1865.

86. Clay and M Leapman, Master Race: The Lebensborn experiment in Nazi Germany, Hodder & Stoughton; UK; page 181; 1995.

87. Gasman, D., The Scientific Origins of National Socialism; American Elsevier; NY; 1971; page 73.

88. Creation: Vol. 18; no. 1; page 9.

89. Life: the science of Biology; Sinauer Associates; 2001; page 13.

90. Wild Earth; Summer Edition; 1991.

91. Alinsky, S., Rules for Radicals; 1971; Opening page dedication.

92. President Harry Truman; Address Before the Attorney General's Conference on Law Enforcement Problems; 2-25-50.

93. Killer Angel; G. Grant; Reformer Press; page 65, 73, 105. Woman's Body; Woman's Right; L. Gordon; Penguin Press; NY, page 332.

94. Killer Angel; George Grant; Reformer Press; page 104.

95. Draper, E., Neo-paganism growing quickly; 6/26/08; Denver Post; www.denverpost.com/commented/ ci_9695062?source=commented

96. Hoogland, J., Calvin College Adam and Eve controversy: The Grand Rapids Press; August 09, 2011.

97. Barna Research; Most Adults Feel Accepted by God, But Lack a Biblical Worldview; August 9, 2005; http://www. barna.org/barna- update/article/5-barna-update/174-most- adults-feel-accepted-by-god-but-lack-a-biblical- worldview?q=worldview.

98. Science and Hebrew Tradition; D. Appleton and Company; New York; 1897; pages 235-236.

99. Hoogland, J., Calvin College Adam and Eve controversy: The Grand Rapids Press; August 09, 2011.

100. New Scientist; June 9, 2001; page 13.

101. The Evolution Cruncher; Vance Ferrell; 2001; page 133.

102. Denver Post; Dec. 13, 1996 Jupiter Probe; K.C. Cole.

103. W. J. Nellis, M. Ross, and N. C. Holmes; Science 269; 1995; 1,249.

104. R. Ouyed, W. Dundamenski, G. Crips, and P. Sutherland; Astrophysical Journal 501; 1995; 367.

105. K. Davies; Distribution of Super Nova Remnants in the Galaxy; 1994; pages 175-184.

107. Heffler, H. and Elsasser, H., Physics of the Galaxy and Interstellar Matter; Springer-Verlag; 1987; Berlin; pages 352–353 and 401–413.

108. See: Creation Ex Nihilo; Dec. 1999; page 8.

109. CESM presentation: 50 Facts versus Biblical Accounts; 2007: visual #'s 45-49.

110. Dr. Purdom, G; Is the Intelligent Design Movement Christian?; The New Answers Book 2; Chapter 13; May 6, 2010.

111. CESM website; FAQ #4; 2011; Http://www.creationministries.org/showpage. aspx?page=8#D4

112. Environmental Geology: An Earth System Science Approach; 1998; page 33.

113. Science News; #279; 1-2-98.

114. Spencer Wells; The Journey of Man: A Genetic Odyssey; 2002. 114. The Origin Of The Species By Means Of Natural Selection or The Preservation Of Favoured Races In The Struggle For Life.
    114.http://wiki.answers.com/Q/What_ was_the_title_Darwin%27s_first

115. CESM presentation: 50 Facts Compared To God's Word; visual 90-92.

116. Dritt, J., Man's earliest beginnings: discrepancies in evolutionary timetables; Proceedings of the Second International Conference on Creationism; Vol. II; 1991; Creation Science Fellowship; PA; pages 73–78.

117. Brinson Bruce, H., Experiment: Fast-Formed Fossils; 9-20-11; http://www.answersingenesis.org/articles/am/v6/n4/fast-formed- fossis.

118. Miller, R., Dobkins, J., 371 Days That Scarred Our Planet; 2009; pages 12-17.

119. Humphreys, R., Physical mechanism for reversals of the earth's magnetic field during the flood; Proceedings of the Second International Conference on Creationism; Vol. II; Creation Science Fellowship; 1991; Pittsburgh, PA; pages 129–142.

120. Williams, A.; 'Oldest' Hominid Footprints Show No Evolution!; September 1, 1993; www.answersingenesis. org/articles/cm/v15/n4/hominid-no-evolution.

121. Baumgardner, J., Measurable 14C in fossilized organic materials: confirming the young earth creation-flood model; Proceedings of the Fifth International Conference on Creationism; Vol. II; Creation Science Fellowship; 2003; Pittsburgh; pages 127–142. Archived at http://globalflood. org/papers/2003ICCc14.html.

122. Austin, S. A., R. Humphreys; The sea's missing salt: a dilemma for evolutionists; Proceedings of the Second International Conference on Creationism; Vol. II; Creation Science Fellowship; 1991; PA; pages 17–33.

123. Milliman, Syvitski; Geomorphic/tectonic control of sediment discharge to the ocean; The Journal of Geology; 1992; Vol. 100; pages 525–544.

Glossary

Apologetics: From the Greek word apologia which means a defense. Christian apologetics provides answers in defense of God's Word.

Atheism: A religious philosophy that matter is all there is, often referred to as atheistic materialism. See Naturalism.

Chromosome: The holder of an organism's genetic information (genes and nucleotide molecules).

COSt: An acronym representing the biblical foundations of God's perfect (C)reation that was corrupted by Adam's (O)riginal Sin which (S)eparated mankind from God (while allowing death to enter the world) requiring that we be † (the Cross of Christ) redeemed with our loving Creator and redeeming Savior, Lord Jesus the Christ.

Darwinism: A theory that, through billions of years of death and struggle, life forms evolved from a common ancestor due to natural selection eliminating the less fit of a species, leaving the stronger variation to carry on the evolving species. **NOTE:** Darwinism is included in our use of the term evolutionism in this writing.

Gene: A biological unit inside of a chromosome. Genes consist of the molecules (A, T, C and G) which compose the rungs of the DNA ladder.

Gene Depletion: The biological principle that mutations or adaptations (variations) are caused by the sorting (re-combination) or loss of the parent's genetic information.

Genome: The complete genetic content of an organism. Most genomes are made of several chromosomes.

Grand Staircase: A series of cliffs in northern Arizona and southern Utah that were left behind by a massive erosion event that removed 130,000 cubic miles of sediments. The steps include the Vermillion Cliffs, the Zion area and Bryce Canyon.

Humanism: A philosophy that mankind is intrinsically good; and relies on human reason, ethics, and justice while rejecting all forms of God-ordained morality and rules. **NOTE:** Secularism is included in our use of this term in this writing.

Intelligent Biblical Design (IBD): A theory that life forms, and many inanimate objects, are too complex to have come about by random accidents so they must have been designed and made by the biblical God.

Intelligent Design (ID): A theory that life forms, and many inanimate objects, are too complex to have come about by random accidents so they must have been designed by a form of intelligence (not necessarily the biblical God).

Kind (biblical): A group of organisms which have brought forth (descended) from the genetic information God created in the original ancestor. **NOTE:** Variations within such a group occur due to the sorting (recombination) or loss (Gene Depletion) of the original genetic data.

Macro-evolution: Darwinian-style change that leads to the origin of new kinds of plants and animals through the addition of new and beneficial genetic data to an existing gene pool.

Micro-evolution: Adaptations or variations within the same kind of plant or animal which lead to kinds bringing forth after their kind. These result from Gene Depletion and are also referred to as micro-adaptations or micro- variations.

Mutation: Changes in the genetic information of an organism that were not present in the parent's gene pool. Mutations come in many forms: deletions, duplications, inversions, substitutions, and more. These result in the loss of functional genetic information.

Naturalism: A religious philosophy, based on the belief matter is all there is, that nothing exists beyond the natural universe. Naturalists assert that the natural laws governing the structure and behavior of the universe came about naturally, not due to a higher power.

Natural Selection: The term given to the fact that organisms best suited to survival in a given environment achieve greater reproductive success and pass their gene pools on to future generations. This acts as God's Quality Assurance Program, usually removing weakened mutants.

Neo-Darwinism: A theory that, through billions of years of time, all life forms evolved due to random genetic mutations adding new and beneficial genetic information to gene pools; followed by Natural Selection eliminating the non-mutant, leaving the improved mutant to carry on the evolving species. **NOTE:** Neo-Darwinism is included in our use of the term Darwinism and evolutionism in this writing.

Occam's razor: The principle that the simplest answer is, other things being equal, generally better than more complex explanations.

Panspermia (Transpermia): The hypothesis life on earth originated elsewhere in the universe and was brought to earth by comets, meteors, aliens of some other unknown source, seeding the planet with living organisms which then began the macro-evolutionary process.

Science (empirical): Knowledge derived from the repeatable observations of existing evidence.

    a) **Historical science** is mankind's attempt to take present processes and apply them to events that occurred in the non-observable past.

    b) **Operational science** is knowledge derived from the repeated studies of observable evidences. This has led to many great inventions and discoveries such as cars, airplanes, antibiotics, laptop computers, etc.

Real Science (Russ's term): see Operational science.

Uniformitarianism: The principle that the present is the key to the past; that things tend to operate in a uniform manner. This is the key to modern day old-earth beliefs: that processes observed today are basically the same as they have been since the earth began.

A

abortion, 62, 114, 117, 119, 120, 210
Abraham Lincoln, 133, 137, 139, 141,
  178, 218
adaptations, 71, 72, 73, 74, 77, 111,
  180, 181, 184, 234, 235
African Eve, 184
Age of Reason, 136
Alexander Hamilton, 132
Alinsky, 119, 120, 157, 231
Ambulocetus, 94
amino acids, 52, 68, 69
amphibian, 93, 199
ancestors, 92, 105, 184
Ancient River, 40, 41
Anthropic Principle, 8, 174, 175, 176
antibiotics,, 106, 236
apes, 89, 99, 100, 102, 108
apologetics, 206, 209, 211, 234
Arcturus, 171
Ardipithecus, 102
atheism, 23, 113
atoms, 28
Australopithecus, 100
axiom, 67, 78

B

bacteria, 37, 38, 51, 54, 69, 76, 78, 79,
  80, 81, 84, 86, 96, 106
Barna, 160, 232
beneficial, 72, 75, 76, 77, 78, 79, 80, 81,
  82, 83, 84, 86, 105, 106, 107, 180,
  235

Betelgeuse, 171
biblical worldview, 10, 31, 38, 54, 149,
  159, 160, 205, 206, 207, 208, 209,
  210, 211
Big Bang, 15, 16, 17, 18, 19, 66, 87, 170,
  172, 173
Bill of Rights, 129, 132, 133, 134
biochemical, 90, 91
Biology, 65, 66, 112, 115, 228, 230, 231
bipedal, 97
birds, 74, 94, 97, 98, 99, 176, 199
Block One Studios, 47
Borglum, 178
Bryce Canyon, 46, 234

C

C-14, 28, 29, 30, 31, 52, 190
Calvin College, 152, 161, 231, 232
Calvin Coolidge, 142
Cambrian Explosion, 92
Canis Majoris, 171
Canyons, 48, 192
Capitol Building, 134, 138, 139
Carbon, 28, 31, 44, 166, 190, 199, 202,
  203, 226
carbon dating, 28, 29, 30, 96
Carboniferous, 190
Case Law, 146, 147
catastrophe, 60, 194
Cedar Mountain, 45, 46
Charles Darwin, 65, 73, 93, 101, 114,
  116
Charles Eliot, 146
chimpanzee, 89
Chromosome, 108, 109, 184, 234
Civil War, 139
Coal, 188
college, 5, 17, 23, 65, 70, 86, 112, 115,
  123, 159, 161, 209, 210, 212
Colorado River, 20, 40, 211
comets, 168, 169, 236
Community Organizer, 119
complex, 16, 17, 28, 58, 69, 75, 76, 86,
  108, 177, 178, 179, 234, 235
Constitution, 123, 129, 130, 131, 132,
  133, 134, 138, 142, 147, 220
Continental Drift, 6, 55, 57, 59
Convergent evolution, 91
corrupted, 1, 3, 9, 10, 15, 28, 37, 62, 86,
  121, 127, 135, 153, 158, 161, 163,
  165, 195, 205, 213, 234
cosmic, 28, 29, 174, 195, 198
Creationism, 162, 163, 226, 227, 233

D

Darwinism, 3, 5, 10, 11, 12, 13, 14, 16,
  47, 50, 62, 63, 65, 66, 67, 69, 70, 71,
  72, 74, 75, 76, 77, 78, 80, 81, 84, 85,
  86, 87, 88, 90, 91, 92, 93, 94, 95, 96,
  97, 99, 100, 101, 102, 103, 105, 107,
  108, 109, 110, 111, 112, 113, 115,
  116, 117, 118, 121, 146, 148, 152,
  153, 157, 160, 180, 181, 183, 206,
  207, 208, 209, 227, 228, 229, 230,
  231, 234, 235, 242

natural law, 132
Natural Selection, 7, 75, 77, 80, 81, 83, 84, 85, 86, 90, 95, 96, 106, 146, 180, 185, 227, 228, 231, 233, 235
Naturalism, 3, 11, 14, 16, 47, 62, 68, 111, 113, 234, 235
Nature journal, 89
Nazism, 115
Neanderthal Man, 100, 102
Neanderthals, 100
Neo-Marxist, 119
neutron, 22, 175
New Scientist, 17, 167, 226, 232
Noah, 13, 52, 53, 54, 128, 182, 184, 185, 186, 194, 195, 196, 197, 198, 199, 200, 201, 203, 211, 226, 227, 242, 243
nucleotide, 68, 234
Nylon, 78

O

observations, 17, 18, 73, 74, 76, 77, 86, 102, 153, 180, 236
Occam's razor, 28, 31, 37, 44, 57, 59, 235
oceans, 59, 60, 61, 66, 87, 175, 183, 202, 203
oil, 20, 22, 30, 202, 203
Old Earth, 148, 183, 226, 242
old-earth, 4, 5, 10, 11, 12, 14, 15, 19, 20, 24, 27, 32, 33, 34, 35, 36, 37, 38, 39, 40, 41, 42, 43, 51, 58, 63, 65, 66, 113, 152, 155, 156, 157, 158, 159, 161, 168, 194, 205, 236
ontogeny, 109
open system, 85
Operational science, 110, 236
ORFan genes, 89
origin, 67, 68, 69, 70, 73, 87, 229, 235
Owen, 51

P

pastors, 126, 127, 134, 136, 155, 159, 160, 206, 209, 210
Patrick Henry, 131
Patterson, 94, 229
peat, 189
petroglyphs, 52
phyla, 92

phylogeny, 109
Planned Parenthood, 120
plasmid, 79
plasmid transfer, 79
Plate Tectonics, 6, 55
point mutations, 81
Pollux, 171
Polonium, 43
Polystrate, 191
post-Flood, 61, 182, 188, 191
preserved, 199
Primates, 7, 97, 99, 103
Progressive Creation, 162, 163
prophecy, 21, 38
protein, 69, 79, 106
proton, 22, 175
Public Education, 116, 148, 242
public schools, 9, 12, 63, 116, 117, 123, 145, 147, 148, 149
Punctuated Equilibrium, 95

R

radioisotope, 24, 25, 27, 31
Radiometric, 6, 24
Recapitulation, 109, 115
Red Butte, 45, 46
religious clause, 133, 134
Resistance, 105
Revolutionary War, 127, 130, 132, 135
Richardson, 109
Roche Limit, 168
Roger Baldwin, 146
Ronald Reagan, 151
Roosevelt, 143, 178
Rules for Radicals, 119, 157, 231

S

Sanger, 120, 121
Savior, 3, 5, 9, 10, 15, 38, 63, 65, 127, 147, 150, 157, 158, 159, 162, 165, 166, 167, 173, 194, 205, 213, 214, 215, 216, 234, 242
Science Magazine, 17
Science News, 101, 230, 232
Second Law, 16, 17, 18, 85
Secularism, 161, 234
serpent, 53
seth, 184
Sexual Revolution, 118

The Calling

The calling of *Creation, Evolution & Science Ministries* is to rebuild the biblical foundations by teaching about Creation, evolution and *age of the earth* issues and exposing false, anti-biblical teachings in order to provide a reason for the hope that is in the heart of every true Believer in, and every true seeker of, our Creator, Judge and redeeming Savior, Lord Jesus the Christ.

Our messages include: *Noah's Ark & Dinosaurs* (God's Word is true, word for word, cover to cover); *If the Foundations Be Destroyed* (Biblical Creation is the foundation of the Gospel & the USA's freedoms); *Science versus Darwinism in the Textbooks* (this caused a secular university to launch a class attacking Russ and Creation); *An Old Earth or A Global Flood?; Facts Compared To The Bible; Six-Day Formation of Grand Canyon: Evil Fruit of Old Earth Beliefs: Microscopic Man, Astronomical God*; *A Pinch of Leaven Can Spoil Your Faith*; *False Christs Shall Arise*; and *Public Education Menticide*. These can be combined to make world class, life-changing camps, conferences and church events.

We also employ *Grand Canyon* and the *Grand Staircase* to reveal the truth of God and His Word. We do this through our teachings and our Bible-based rim tours to these areas.

Visit **www.CreationMinistries.Org** to learn more!

Illustrations from Russ Miller's
Noah's Ark & Dinosaurs and
Endowed by their Creator activity books.

Russ Miller's books; multi-session DVD's (which he encourages people to copy and give away); descriptions of his church, camp and conference messages; Grand Canyon and Grand Staircase tour information; answers to frequently asked questions and much more can be found at: **www.CreationMinistries.Org**

Russ has written four books with co-author Jim Dobkins:
The Theft of America's Heritage
The Darwinian Delusion
371 Days That Scarred Our Planet
The Submerging Church.

Russ has also written and illustrated two informative activity books, ***Noah's Ark and Dinosaurs*** and
Endowed by their Creator- America's Christian Heritage.
These and more can be found in our online bookstore at
www.CreationMinistries.Org

Made in the USA
San Bernardino, CA
04 June 2018